Counting Frogs
& Eating Crow

David Whitely

Tml good wishes to Linda,

Mary Cook —

My Life in Radio
by Mary Cook

www.creativebound.com

Published by Creative Bound Inc.
Box 424 Carp, Ontario
Canada, K0A 1L0
(613) 831-3641

ISBN 0-921165-85-4
Printed and bound in Canada

Book design by Wendelina O'Keefe
Cover photo from *Fifty-Five Plus*, October-November 1992

National Library of Canada Cataloguing in Publication Data

Cook, Mary, 1932-
     Counting frogs and eating crow: my life in radio / Mary Cook.

ISBN 0-921165-85-4

     1. Cook, Mary, 1932- 2. Radio broadcasters--Canada--Biography.
I. Title.

PN1991.4.C63A3 2003   791.44'028'092   C2003-906031-4

Many people have contributed to whatever success and longevity I enjoy today as a broadcaster.

Alan Maitland guided and taught me everything I know about reaching a listener. His belief in me was a constant inspiration, and he and his wife Connie became lifelong friends.

And had it not been for my producer Shirley Gobeil, my Depression stories would never have been told, nor would there have been eight books published previous to this one. I owe a great debt to Shirley who always knew what the listener wanted to hear, and who had a deep sense of loyalty to both the audience and those who worked under her leadership.

And finally, I will be forever grateful to the countless readers and listeners who have inspired me with their interest in my written and spoken word. Their constant feedback has been a great source of encouragement to me.

And so it is with deep gratitude to Alan and Connie Maitland, Shirley Gobeil, and my listeners and readers that I lovingly dedicate this book.

Contents

The Right Place at the Right Time

A Funny Thing Happened...

The Pebble Effect

Growing
Into the Job

In the Beginning

Everyone has a point at which time his or her life takes a turn. Mine took on a new spin during my last year of high school. Today, so many years later, I often wonder where I would be had I not had teachers who expected great things from me, a mother who prodded me forward, and the gift of enough nerve and audacity to set myself a bit apart from my peers.

Coming into high school fresh off the farm just after the start of the Second World War, I was scared out of my wits, possessing not a shred of daring. Unlike the one-room school I had attended in the country, here there were no older sister and three brothers to shield me from the stares of the town kids who dressed differently and walked with a swagger in their saddle shoes and rolled-down white socks. Worse, the girls from town wore store-bought underwear, which I was quick to notice that first day in gym class—unlike my underpinnings which were made from bleached flour bags that bore traces of "Pride of the Valley" across the seat.

It would be safe to say that for the first year I was nothing more than one of "those poor country kids who dress funny and have headcheese sandwiches in their lunch." But by the time that first year was over, and I saw with relief that I had made it into the next grade, I made up my mind that if I was going to survive my remaining high school years, I would have to do more to make myself fit in with the crowd.

To this day I have no idea what possessed me, but with a burst of boldness I didn't know I possessed, I offered myself up for a part in the school play. To my horror, I found myself in the lead role.

Once the initial shock wore off, and I came to grips with what I had rashly done, I discovered I was in my element. I remember vividly the title of that play: The Prince Who Was a Pauper. The prince was a handsome young man, a couple of years my senior, and we melded together in our roles as if we had been born to the stage. The success of that play gave me a burst of self-confidence, and I decided high school was not going to be half bad after all, and I would get out of it only what I put into it.

From that moment on, my high school years became one big long and happy interval in my life where I excelled in anything that wasn't academic. I blossomed in the Glee Club where I was put in the alto section, and I admit now, so many years later, that I often faked it, unless I was standing beside someone with a very strong voice who could keep me on key. I edited the school newspaper, starred at track and field, and became a cheerleader and Students' Council representative. My marks were abysmal, but I had a good and glorious span of years as a high school student. I simply had no time to spend on schoolwork! And I managed to pass each year, to the complete astonishment of everyone.

It was during my last year that my English teacher, Helen

Mullett, approached me about a letter she had received from one of the editors of an Ottawa newspaper. He was looking for a final-year student who might be interested in "stringing" for the paper. English was one of the few subjects I truly enjoyed (for some reason, geometry was another). I snapped up the offer and received the immense remuneration of five cents a published word. It is to be noted that I didn't get a cent for anything I wrote that the editors didn't see fit to print!

Fortunately for me, my parents had given up the farm just after my first year in high school, and so I was now on the scene of any Carleton Place action. News items came easily; I saw things to write about around every corner and on just about any street in town. I had a bicycle, and with notepad tucked into a pocket and a ten-dollar camera on a strap over my shoulder, I set out to be the hottest reporter ever to emerge from the Ottawa Valley.

The first day my name appeared under an article, I was so overjoyed (as was my English teacher) that I cut it out and glued it to the front of *The Admirable Creighton*, which was the book we were reading in English class at the time. And so began my love of the written word.

It was also during that last year in high school, after my name had appeared on articles in the city paper, that I got a phone call from Frank Ryan, the owner of a new radio station in the nation's capital. He was looking for someone to broadcast from the local county fairs in the Ottawa Valley. Would I be interested?

Before he could change his mind, I went to his office to find out exactly what a radio broadcaster did at county fairs. I barely knew what a radio was! Our farm had had no electricity, and the small radio we bought when we moved to town was able to receive about three stations.

The only thing I remember about the interview with Frank Ryan was that he had a genuine Holstein cowhide-covered couch in his office, which just about made me ill to look at, since my deep love for farm animals and my vivid imagination had me picturing the demise of the poor cow who had given up her hide! However, common sense prevailed, and with absolutely no knowledge of broadcasting (or even what a microphone looked like) and with no idea what kind of stories the man was interested in, I accepted the job. Like my newspaper responsibilities, I could work this job in with my high school studies.

And so it was that the ground was laid for what would ultimately become five-plus decades in the world of radio broadcasting. It would be nice to say I jumped with both feet into the big world of writing and broadcasting just as I was handed my high school diploma. But here my road took some more turns and twists, and although I continued to write spasmodically, the private radio job ended with my final day in high school.

Just a Blip on the Screen

Although nothing more than a blip on my screen many years ago, had I not taken on a new challenge after my high school graduation, I realize now that I would never have met the man I would marry.

The Rexall Drug Store in Carleton Place was the busiest in town. I knew the owner well, and was a good friend of his daughter. I had finished school, and my past writing and broadcasting, as spasmodic as they had been, still wetted my appetite enough that I was most reluctant to branch off into any other line of work. However, I was approached by the parent Rexall Company and given a challenge I thought I could meet, and it had enough excitement attached to it that I even thought I might make a career out of it.

The company wanted to train me to become a registered cosmetician and introduce a new line of cosmetics, which was being brought into their chain from England and stocked in various stores in this part of the country. The cosmetics were a beautiful product called Tiffany, and it was my job to put the line into the stores and see that it was promoted. I had "done" about four stores between Ottawa and the town of Picton when I was called to Toronto for a meeting where I would be given more instructions and information on the line. It was on that trip to Toronto that a promise sidelined me into the city of Peterborough, and it was there I met the man who would turn out to be my life partner.

With marriage, that job came to an end. But just around the corner would be other opportunities and challenges, and a lifelong career that would put me back in front of a microphone.

Was it fate that had me deviate from my route, or had an angel already landed on my shoulder? The same angel I feel has been with me so many times, opening doors, encouraging me to look beyond the minute at hand, and leading me to opportunities that many years ago I would never have thought possible.

Meeting Big Wally

Walker Stores Limited was a chain of junior department stores scattered throughout Ontario. The
chain was owned by Gordon MacKay, a large wholesale company
located in Toronto, and each store had a manager who was
assigned to the location by head office. Walker Stores in Carleton
Place had been there for many, many years, and was a favourite
family store in which you could buy everything from quality
linens to baby's wear to thread and lady's fashions.

The manager in my hometown of Carleton Place and I were
good friends, and he was being transferred to another location.
We used to joke that Walker Stores moved managers like you
would move checkers on a board. The managers never knew when
they were being moved, or to what community.

In my friend's place, a man from Peterborough was being sent to
Carleton Place. Since I was driving to Toronto, my Carleton Place
friend asked me if I would stop in at the Peterborough store and
introduce myself. He understood the man being sent to Eastern

Ontario wasn't at all pleased with the move, and perhaps if he was made to feel welcome, he would be more receptive to coming to a small town after working in a city the size of Peterborough.

I was halfway through Peterborough when I remembered my promise, and I actually gave consideration to continuing on without stopping to give a welcome to this new manager, whom I was sure would be just like all the other Walker Store managers I knew: middle aged or better, portly, receding hairline or none at all, and married with a raft of kids! Since I was young, single and still looking, I was reasonably sure the new manager heading my way would be ineligible and never meet my criteria for a possible future relationship. That's how self-centred I was back then. However, my puritan upbringing told me a promise was a promise, and I turned around and headed for the business core of Peterborough, and Walker Stores.

When I entered the store, a group of men in business suits stood near the purse counter talking, and I gave them the once over, trying to decide which one was the new manager heading my way. I mentally dismissed the youngest of the lot, mainly because he was obviously the youngest, but also because he had all his hair, was over six feet tall, and didn't look like any of the Walker Store managers I knew.

I asked a salesperson where I could find the man who was being transferred to Carleton Place. She said "that would be Mr. Cook," and she pointed in the general direction of the group of men. I headed over and asked "Mr. Cook?" Fully expecting one of the older, portly men to respond, I was thunderstruck when the tall, good-looking guy turned and acknowledged he was Wally Cook.

I can't remember the conversation, but I probably welcomed him to Carleton Place and made some other inane statement while mentally adding his name to my list of prospects for the future! Of course, I still didn't know if he was married with a batch of kids. Later on, he told me that his comment to his fellow workers was "My God, she even has freckles on her lips."

Well, within days, Wally Cook moved to Carleton Place and we reconnected. Within three months we were engaged, and within six we were married! That was in 1952 and, as the saying goes, 'the rest is history.'

Marrying Wally was probably the best decision I ever made. Although I knew with his job that regular moves anywhere in the province of Ontario were always a possibility, little did I know that each move we took was like putting together another piece in a large, colourful jigsaw puzzle, with each piece adding to the mosaic of my life.

• • •

Tillsonburg, in Southern Ontario, was deep in the heart of tobacco country, its population a mixture of transplanted Americans, Europeans and natives to the community whose ancestors had built the town and who were firmly established on its social rungs. I was sure they would have little time for an Ottawa Valley farm girl. A quick assessment told me my chances of doing any broadcasting or writing were minuscule. I was prepared to hate the place, and knew I would expire from sheer loneliness.

It was in this town that I learned a valuable lesson. I learned that you get out of a community exactly what you put into it. It was a lesson I would carry the rest of my life.

Within a week, Wally and I had joined the Presbyterian Church, and I was asked to direct a one-act play for the local Little Theatre and to sub in one of the bridge clubs. In this early flurry of activity, I was also elected president of the Badminton Club. I must digress and explain the latter accomplishment: Wally was an excellent badminton player. And since he had moved to this new town several months before I could join him, he was well established in the club. Badminton was not one of my long suits. It didn't take long for club members to realize that. I was flattered when they asked me to be the new president; however, not too many nights had passed before I determined why I'd been given this honour...I was the poorest player in the club. As president, I was busy enough that there was little time for me to actually get on the courts!

It wasn't hard to grow into the town and fall in love with its people, so diversified and accepting. However, the fact remained that Wally had the kind of job where without more than a two-day notice he could be transferred to another location. This was the case that saw us move from the town I had grown to love and right into a much larger community.

Although not unlike the small town we had lived in previously, Sarnia was thought of as a city. It didn't take me long to find out it had a radio station, and with more nerve than a canal horse, I took myself down to the main business core and offered up myself for employment. Certainly my credentials left a lot to be desired: a stringer for a newspaper, doing sporadic broadcasts from small county fairs. To this day I have no idea what impressed the station owners, but I was hired on the spot. To be given a full hour, midday, was beyond my wildest dreams, until I realized that not only did I have to prepare the entire show, I had to sell the advertising, write the ads and work them into the program!

As a total stranger to the city, I knew my job would be a formidable one. But I possessed a naive attitude that convinced me

Mary Cook • 18

that if I worked hard and put on a great show, selling spots for the broadcast would be a cinch. It certainly wasn't my idea, but the manager decided to call the show "Tea Time with Mary Cook," which on reflection gave the performance a quaint and warm tone, but did little to convince the local business community to spend their dollars on a one-minute spot!

I have never worked so hard in my life, before or since, but somehow I managed to find enough sponsors to get the show rolling. Filling the hour with news and interesting items was the easy part. Learning to write the ads, keep the copy within a 60-second time frame, and cram about eight of them into the hour-long show, proved to be more of a challenge.

In a smaller community, any on-air personality during the mid-fifties soon finds herself in the centre of the action whether she wants it or not. It was expected that I would commentate fashion shows, judge soap box races, open bazaars and do any number of other civic duties, mainly because there were few other resource people to call on. And, of course, to refuse an invitation was to risk losing a listener, who might also be a sponsor.

I was fast wearing out, and the show, as popular as it was, started to take its toll on me. I have always said I travel through this life with an angel on my shoulder. And it was that angel who intervened. Wally received notice of yet another transfer. With less than a week's notice we were to be in Windsor, Ontario, and I, with equal parts of relief and sadness, had to tender my resignation.

I was sure that my career in radio was over. After all, Windsor was a big city, with well-established broadcasters. There would be no room for an Ottawa Valley girl, whose sole experience lay in spots at the county fair and hosting a show with a homespun name.

The Gift of a Mentor

Windsor, we were told, was a blue-collar city. The motor industry was ensconced there, as were many related businesses. Hiram Walker Distillers was a massive plant I passed on my way to the downtown core the first day I went to the city's largest department store, where Wally had been posted as merchandise manager. The stores he had managed previously would all fit into the downstairs of this multi-floored building overlooking the Detroit River. The C. H. Smiths store was unionized, with the staff numbering well over two hundred.

As I drove from one end of the city to the other to explore our new surroundings, the aroma of malt and fermented grain from Hiram Walker permeated the air and covered that part of the city with the sweet smell of its spirited products. I often thought this would a poor spot for an alcoholic to live if he was trying to get off the bottle!

The Ford Motor Company, another of the city's largest industries, was the major employer, and when we moved to Windsor, I learned just how dependent the economy was on the large blue-collar workforce. But there was another side to Windsor. The arts community was thriving, Windsor University was a vibrant place of study, and the lakeshore boasted luxurious homes, some sitting on reclaimed land, but all with beautifully manicured lawns attesting to the prosperity of a large portion of the population.

Wally and I found a small but adequate two-storey home across from a large Catholic secondary school, and we settled in. The urge to become part of Windsor was strong. I studied the *Windsor Star* every day to see if there could be a place for me to fit in and become part of the city. I devoured the announcement columns, and one day (Providence, I call it) members of the public were invited to attend a Cancer Society meeting. There were countless other organizations begging for volunteers, but I chose the Cancer Society, hoping that I could not only help out its cause, but that it would give me the opportunity to meet some of Windsor's movers and shakers. If this was going to be my home, then I wanted to be part of the city in every sense of the word.

As it turned out, the meeting was held at a local bank after hours, the same bank where Wally and I had our meagre savings. There were perhaps a dozen people there, and most of them were men—all in business suits, with polished shoes and perfectly matching shirts and ties. Isn't it funny that after all these years I can remember what I wore that night? Perhaps it is because the man who offered me a seat commented on my dress, noting that purple was his favourite colour. I liked him instantly.

The man introduced himself as Alan Maitland, and I almost fell off my chair! Was this really the Alan Maitland I had been listening to on CBC for years? When I asked him if he was "Fireside Al," and the same Alan Maitland from "Maitland Manor," a program that had aired out of Toronto, he admitted he was.

That evening, both Alan and I accepted executive positions with the Cancer Society—he in promotion, and I as extension chairman, whose job it was to go out into Essex County and the rural areas surrounding Windsor and start branches for the Cancer Society. Our two jobs would meld together, the success of both depending on each other.

Over coffee after the meeting, Al told me he was program director at CBE, the Windsor affiliate station for the Canadian Broadcasting Corporation, and before the meeting was over we made plans to use his position to promote public meetings throughout the area. Alan Maitland knew all about reaching a listening audience, and together we drew up a list of possible interviews of people well-regarded in the city whom I would interview as extension chairman. (Back in the 1950s, we never thought calling a woman a chairman was politically incorrect.) We chose a two-hour phone-in as a good place to start, and a city councillor as our first guest.

Even then, the wheels of the CBC were slow to turn, and schedules had to be arranged and programming reorganized to make way for such a long insert into the calendar. I was impatient, and still finding it lonely living in my first big city. I longed to fill in the wide gaps in my life, and in a fit of impatience, I accepted a position as a fashion consultant with one of Detroit's leading stores, Saks Fifth Avenue.

One of the country's most prestigious high-fashion stores, Saks gave me a good look at the cutthroat business of commissioned sales, and the class distinctions (indicative of what part of Detroit you called home) and race barriers that marked that period of time in America. Of course, I didn't live in any part of Detroit, and taking the Detroit-Windsor tunnel every day to the store was a challenge for someone who wouldn't previously have dreamt of going "under a river" to save her soul! At the outset, I lived in dread that the whole thing would collapse or that I would be over-come by the gas fumes of the other vehicles, as a steady flow of commuters passed from one country to the next with ease, all via this underpass.

I took my mind off the trek to the Fisher Building, where Saks was located, by trying to get into the minds and the lives of the other passengers on the bus. Who were they? Where were they going? What were their families like? Although I didn't realize it at the time, my lifelong curiosity about other people would prove one of my most valuable assets in the years ahead.

• • •

When I least expected it, after I had considered the idea of a two-hour phone-in for the Essex County Cancer Society shelved, the call came from Alan Maitland to say the time had been booked and the municipal representative lined up. All I had to do was arrive at the studio and field the questions from the listening audience for two hours. In my naïveté, I assumed the program couldn't be that much different from what I had been doing with "Tea Time with Mary Cook" in private radio in Sarnia.

Problems started the moment I stepped off the elevator. Always early for every appointment, I arrived long before the scheduled broadcast. There was a new technician on the job, I was told, and I would have to man my own microphone, as well as handle the phone calls.

As the clock started to tick down, the municipal representative was still to appear. With seconds to go before air time, it became apparent he had no intention of surfacing. For a solid day, the phone-in had been promoted on air, and so there was no alternative but to go into the studio alone, give a preamble, open up the phone lines and let the chips fall where they may!

Alan Maitland had given me enough brochures and Cancer Society information to provide me with armchair reading for a week. Unfortunately, I had had no time to look it over. Flying blind, I prayed for the wisdom to handle what had been dumped in my lap, and what in my mind was quickly developing into a calamity. I caught a glimpse of Alan on the other side of the glass. He gave me a "thumbs up" and then calmly walked out of the control room. I never laid eyes on him again until the show was over.

Once again, that angel was on my shoulder. Calls poured in, the majority from listeners who had first-hand experience with either cancer or the Cancer Society. A very few were questions, most of which I could not answer; however, I somehow had the sense to take names and numbers with the promise of a return call.

As luck would have it, the show that day was being monitored by CBC's head office in Toronto. Had I known that at the time, I doubt I could have carried off a two-hour show, unprepared as I was. Back then, it was common practice for head office in Toronto to monitor shows across the country. It was the network's way of keeping a finger on the pulse of the stations. The phone call that would change my life came the next day.

Baptism by Fire

Windsor was a hot and humid place to be in the summer. Air conditioning was still a luxury. That morning, I thought I was going to melt. The phone rang early, as I was trying to figure out what I could wear to work at my job at Saks that wouldn't look like I had slept in it all night. At first, I thought it was a man on the phone, but since I had never heard of a man named Helen, I had to assume the voice belonged to a woman.

There was no small talk as she came right to the point: "I'm Helen James from the CBC in Toronto and we are prepared to offer you a job." At first I thought she was offering some sort of office position, until she started talking about my being on-air every day at noon hour, five days a week. When the impact of her offer finally reached the nerve centre of my brain, I had no idea what to say. I needn't have worried; Helen James did all the talking.

Arrangements were made to have me fly to Toronto for an interview. At the network's expense, I boarded an old propeller-driven

Viscount, and took off on my first plane ride, vowing that if I got off the thing alive, I would kiss the ground and walk back to Windsor! The anxiety over the job interview paled in comparison to the fright I felt rattling around in the clouds, instilling in me a fear of flying, which to this day no amount of air miles can erase.

"Do you always talk like that?" was one of the first questions Helen James asked me. "Like what?" I asked. "Well, with that drawl or twang. Where does it come from?" She and Helen Carscallen, another CBC executive, looked me up and down, and declared I would fit the bill if they could do something about what we determined was a decided Ottawa Valley accent. They had me say berries, cows, bank and onions, and then one slapped her thigh, the other her desk, and they both laughed as if they would fall off their chairs.

Of course, I was still gainfully employed at Saks Fifth Avenue, but the idea of not having to commute under the Detroit River was enough to convince me to accept the CBC offer. On signing the contract, I became the tenth female commentator for the CBC in Canada.

I know now that Alan Maitland had more than a little to do with my being asked to take over the commentator's job in Windsor. According to Carscallen, my mandate was "to be the eyes and ears of the housewife in my listening area." With the exception of having to read a weekly—and lengthy—letter from various correspondents in faraway lands, the entire five days of programming was my responsibility. There would be no researcher, secretary, librarian or assistant. I was in this alone.

There was virtually no taping ahead of programming back then; broadcasts were done live in the studio. I marvel today at my nerve, thinking I could walk into a woman's commentary position with so little experience. But if nothing else, I was passionate about succeeding at this job.

With Alan Maitland's help, I drew up ideas on how I could capture my share of a radio audience that at that point tuned mainly to the Detroit stations. It wouldn't be easy. Making lists of every organization in the city of Windsor, municipal representatives and those of other government agencies, schools and industries, I sent out dozens of letters of introduction. I wasn't prepared for the response. I soon had more "leads" and interviews lined up than I knew what to do with. Potential interviewees were all delighted at the prospect of free publicity for their particular interests. The challenge was to fit every worthy cause into my schedule, keep interest high, and not alienate as a listener anyone whose agenda didn't fit my mandate.

Wally bought me a second-hand Hillman, black with red leather interior, which I soon discovered didn't like Canadian winters. A new tape recorder and a briefcase, and I was ready. Before I had a chance to even think about my inaugural program, word came from Toronto that someone would be arriving on my doorstep to see what could be done about my Ottawa Valley twang.

The gentleman who "came to my rescue" had a decidedly cultured English accent of his own. Despite that, I soon discovered he had been raised in a suburb of London, Ontario. Learning to say bank instead of *baynk*, and berries instead of *burries*, where to pause for emphasis in a sentence, and how to pace my dialogue for impact, were all part of the intense lessons I endured. Within two weeks, there was a noticeable change in my speech, although it could never be said that I lost my twang altogether!

It's funny now, so many years later, that I have no recollection of the content of my first program, but I can remember just about everything else that happened when I stepped off the elevator at CBE studios on Pelissier Street.

Alan Maitland was poised with a camera, and captured me emerging in a new navy sack dress which was the rage in the late 1950s, complete with a white straw hat and white gloves that came to just below my elbow. Today, I would dress like that for a tea with the Governor General. Back then, I thought I was the epitome of a professional—just what would be expected of a CBC commentator.

Everyone connected with the studio was on board to welcome me, and with a few minutes to spare before show time, Alan gave me instructions. He talked about the timer, the red button, the technician who would be giving me hand signals... I looked at him as if he was from another planet. I had no idea what he was talking about! Within minutes I would be in the studio, with an announcer to get me into the show, and then I would be flying solo! There was no time to panic.

The announcer assigned to me was as blonde as a lily, with shoulders as wide as a stand of trees, and a personality to match. His name was Alan Hamel, and he had a few more months under his belt with the CBC than I had, but he had enough assurance for both of us. We sailed through the show and became instant friends. Little did either of us know at the time that he would go on to fame and fortune as "that Canadian guy who married Suzanne Somers" from Hollywood.

Windsor was ready for a young and eager female broadcaster. Within weeks, I was established and fielding interviews on everything from children's health issues to union concerns to school matters.

Windsor's proximity to the American border also gave me the

opportunity of interviewing many famous stars who made Detroit a port of call. Most worked out well. Some didn't.

Sophie Tucker was a headliner at a place called the Elmwood Casino, and I decided she would be a great guest. She would be the first of many interviews I conducted with people who were famous enough to make headlines in the dailies.

Heading out with my tape recorder, I was surprised to find Sophie much older than her publicity pictures. In a raspy voice, she ordered me to sit down while she finished her morning coffee. Wearing a flowing red silk gown, she settled in at a table and indicated she was ready.

I asked what I thought were pertinent questions, and every answer I got was laced with the kind of profanity I would expect from a salty old sailor on the docks. We talked for about an hour, but it took far less time than that for me to realize I couldn't use a word of the interview on the radio. Today, it would be accepted. In the 1950s, it was inadmissible.

It was to be just one of the few times in my long career with the CBC that I was unable to air an interview because of its content. But that interview with Sophie Tucker taught me a valuable lesson: determine quickly where the interview is going; if you have to question if it's appropriate, it probably isn't.

• • •

September of 1956 was a memorable month for me and for Wally. Not only did I begin what would turn out to be almost 50 years with the CBC, but the adoption agency called to say the baby we had been awaiting for close to four years had arrived. Richard John Cook was 10 weeks old when we took him home; he would be the first of three children we would adopt over the next six years.

Richard often came with me on interviews and to the studio. The rest of the time, he was in the care of a wonderful Scottish nanny who dressed him in kilts and who also became great friends with Wally's father, who had come to live with us shortly after we were married. Grampa was from Wick in Scotland, and he and Granny Houston got along famously. Richard's first words had a Scottish burr to them.

Broadcasting daily was a challenge. It's safe to say that 10 to 15 hours of every day were spent getting the show ready. The next day it would start all over again.

I worried constantly that the opportunity for good programs would dry up, or that I wouldn't be able to build a solid listening audience. Alan Maitland led me through my concerns and gave me valuable advice that I use to this day: "Building a listening audience is like building a brick house. You do it one brick at a time. You never alienate your listeners. You take every phone call personally. Your name and telephone number should be available, and you treat every person you meet as if they are important to you, because, remember, they are." I have never forgotten that advice.

Coming up with unique guests for the show was my aim. There weren't as many women in the workforce in those days. Many stayed at home and raised their children, and my mandate was to bring those who listened to the CBC closer to people they would otherwise not have had the opportunity of meeting. As well as attracting a large female segment of the population, I was able to draw a reasonable male audience with the wide scope of programming I strived for. It was a challenge to come up with interviews and stories that would appeal to a diversified audience, but it was one of the many things I liked about my role as a broadcaster.

I found stories everywhere. The city and the rural communities were rich with people with tales to tell. Reaching back to my high school reporting days, I used the ideas I had back then for ferreting out interviews with people who had offbeat jobs, interests and backgrounds.

Al Maitland was full of suggestions and worked closely with me. As program director for the Windsor station, he wanted me to succeed as much as I did. He had years on me in this game. One day during a story meeting, Al declared it might be a clever idea for a program if I took my listeners behind the scenes with a Detroit detective...follow him for a day...see what it's like to be on the front lines in a city where the crime rate was increasing almost as fast as its population. We were starting to cut into the Detroit audience. The idea made sense.

That one day developed into several, and in the end, I had what amounted to a documentary. It gave me my first experience at looking at the seedy side of a big city with all its violence and corruption. Those few days left me with a pain in my gut that would take months to erase.

The Ship That Sails

I'd rather drive where sea storms blow,
And be the ship that always failed
To make the ports where it would go,
Than be the ship that never sailed.

John Fiske

Doing hard news stories was a big departure from my previous broadcasting experience with its warm and fluffy content. I was very apprehensive that I would not have the stamina to deal with a darker side of humanity. I wasn't even sure I wanted to try. I was very content with both the content of my work and the listener response to it. Again, Alan Maitland settled the issue in his usual fatherly and professional way, stating, "You will never know until you try. And if you don't try, you may always regret not having brought another dimension to your work." And then he said something I will never forget. "You will never know how you will handle stories with an edge until you tackle them. Failure is not a dirty word."

And so, with more than a little trepidation, I started out on another path. Not to replace the kind of stories I was known for, but to give to my listeners a wider scope of programming.

• • •

Dave was driving an unmarked car when he picked me up at the studio. He was dressed in a business suit, as was his partner. It was a hot day, made hotter in the car because it had no air conditioning. Dave explained briefly what I could expect during the hours ahead. He said petty crime traditionally increased in the hot weather, but he didn't expect anything major to unfold on the streets of downtown Detroit. The radio in the car crackled, but neither detective paid any attention to it. We chatted easily for the better part of an hour, cruising streets that were littered with papers, discarded cigarette boxes and bottles—evidence of another normal night in downtown Detroit. We talked easily about life on the streets as a detective in a big city, how the unexpected was always just around the corner, and how you had to leave the day's events in the office when it was time to go home. Seedy bars lined the street we were on, and I noticed Dave drove with one eye on the road, and the other on the people shuffling along in the heat.

Without any warning, someone flew out a bar door, and landed in a heap on the sidewalk. In a tone I knew meant business, I was ordered to stay in the car and keep the doors locked. The heat was suffocating, but I knew better than to roll down the windows. Within minutes, an ambulance and several police cruisers slammed into the sidewalk, and people began to pour out of the bar. My heart was pounding; I felt I was going to smother. This certainly wasn't what I expected to take back to my listeners. "This could take a while," Dave yelled to me through the window. "I'll wait," I said stupidly. Where would I go if I decided to leave, for heaven's sake?

Someone was wheeled out on a gurney and into the ambulance, and someone else was brought out in handcuffs and pushed into another cruiser. The better part of the morning was over before Dave and his partner piled back into the car. They informed me I had just been witness to the first murder of the day in downtown Detroit. Someone had been shot dead at point-blank range while having a drink at a bar.

On our return to the police station, while the men did their paperwork, I used the time to interview the girl at the front desk. She told me about her first day on the job, and how she almost quit that day when a small child was murdered. "You harden to the things that happen around you, and you have to think of this as just being a job. You can't let it get to you, or you'd never come back." Her interview was the first piece that aired on what would turn out to be a documentary of a day spent riding on the coat-tails of a pair of Detroit detectives.

That day, I discovered there was another side to broadcasting. I couldn't always leave my listeners with a warm glow and in high spirits. Sometimes they would have to hear pieces that weren't so nice and comfortable to listen to.

I hadn't expected the morgue to be a port of call for a detective, but that was our next stop. To this day, I thank my Creator that I was able to choose between actually watching an autopsy or just seeing the rooms in which they were performed. Needless to say,

I opted for the latter. However, I was not to be spared the grue-some details. A doctor had just completed a case, and he explained to me in minute detail why the table had grooves in it and was made of aluminum, and why the smell of formaldehyde just about bowled me over.

An adjoining room housed a full wall of long drawers—a famil-iar sight today on television detective shows. Back then, however, I had no idea what a morgue looked like. Nor did I know each drawer held a body.

An attendant went to one of the drawers and yanked it open to reveal a huge black man, partially covered with a sheet. Dave told me he had been dead for months, and since no one had claimed the body, he was being "defrosted" to be buried in Potter's Field.

I wasn't sure how much more I could take that day. I can remember the suit I wore. It was beige linen, with short sleeves. I hadn't had it long. After that day, no number of dry cleanings, and even machine washings, could get rid of the smell of formalde-hyde. Eventually I had to part with the suit.

Dave suggested we head out again the next morning to cover a court case in which he was a witness. While we were at it, he thought I might like to visit a women's prison. The court case was run-of-the-mill, but the women's prison will forever be engraved in my mind. It was hot and dusty, and smelled of urine. Many of the cells were empty, which Dave said was unusual for that time of year.

We came to a cell where an elderly woman rocked back and forth on a cot, sobbing and clutching an old battered purse. Her feet were bare and her body bony. On top of her kinky black hair sat a white straw hat with a yellow daisy reaching skyward. The hat seemed completely out of place. I asked if I could talk to her inside the cell.

She told me she had been in for three days, waiting for someone to come and post bail. She had stolen a two-dollar wallet from a store and been caught. She cried the entire time I talked to her. I looked pleadingly at Dave, but he just shook his head and said nothing could be done until someone came to bail her out or the courts dealt with the offence. No one knew how long that could be.

By the time I had put in four days following in the footsteps of the two detectives, I was worn out mentally and physically. In the story meeting that followed in Al Maitland's office, we decided to put the pieces together for a documentary. It took hours to sort out the tapes, and I recall it ran in time slots of about ten minutes on four consecutive days. We had tremendous response from CBC listeners, and we decided that although I would always be bringing in the warm human interest stories, we would thereafter try also to air issues that would invariably cause people to think about the cares and concerns of those less fortunate within our listening area. Stories with an edge would become part of my broadcasts, but only a part.

Jamie

Jamie was a handsome young boy, who at eleven years of age, should have had a lifetime ahead of him. But his dreams would be cut short by a massive tumour that was growing in his skull. His immediate future would be filled with long stays in the hospital, unimaginable headaches and endless treatments.

The call came to me from his mother. She had two reasons for getting in touch with me. Firstly, she wanted to publicly thank the Windsor Branch of the Canadian Cancer Society for its continuous support, and secondly, she wanted me to know that Jamie listened to my program every day. It was unusual to have a child tuned in to what was considered to be an adult theme show, but she said he enjoyed listening to the easy banter between Alan Hamel and me. His mother wondered if I would say hello to Jamie on his birthday. She doubted he would live to see another one.

Alan Maitland, who still held a position with the Cancer Society, thought we could go one step further and make a big difference in young Jamie's life. Not only would we wish him happy birthday, we would do it from his home, airing a part of the daily show from his bedside. Only his parents would be party to the surprise awaiting young Jamie.

I remember it as a hot, humid day when a technician and I arrived at the door of the small, neat house. Inside it was cooler, and Jamie's bed had been moved to the living room. He was propped up with mounds of pillows, and I can still remember the bright blue flannelette pyjamas he wore and wondering how he could stand the heat. I will never forget the look of surprise on his face, surpassed only by the sheer joy of having a live radio show broadcast from the side of his bed!

Two far-reaching things came out of that day's programming: firstly, it raised the profile of the Cancer Society, and secondly, it confirmed in my mind the importance of going beyond the studio for stories that would touch the hearts of my listeners. I learned that putting the listener right at the centre of the story was yet another tool in bringing colourful and interesting stories to the air. It was a lesson I would take with me over the next four decades with the CBC.

Best of all, our broadcast that day brought joy to a little boy whose life would be cut short by a devastating illness.

Down to the Salt Mines

Windsor is very much an industrial city. When times are tough, and the economy slow, the place is hit hard and just about everyone feels it. Back in the late 1950s when we lived there, so much depended on the car industry. If it flattened out, local businesses suffered. But one industry always seemed able to ride out the hard times: that was the Canadian Salt Company. Everyone loved salt. It was a thriving business, and a major industry for the city.

The Canadian Salt Company had hit a milestone the year I started with the CBC. It had gone something like three years without a serious accident—a remarkable feat when one considered the dangers of working more than 1000 feet under the ground.

The fact that the Canadian Salt Company had reached this pinnacle in worker safety was a big story as far as Alan Maitland was concerned. At a story meeting, it was decided I would be the one to go underground and spend a day in the salt mines. He thought the story had enough merit to make it onto the national network.

All I needed to know was that the site for recording the story would be more than 1000 feet underground, with much of it right under the Detroit River, for heaven's sake. I flew immediately into panic mode! Was he mad? Did he actually expect me, the one who suffered from severe claustrophobia, to go deep into the bowels of the earth to spend several hours in a place where I was convinced the law of averages would run out and this would be the day the Canadian Salt Company would break its safety record? He did indeed! Not only that, he had already assigned a technician to accompany me, since he didn't want to rely on my tape recorder because of the story's potentially national scope.

I made one request. I would go underground only if my husband Wally was allowed to go with me. Once we all got clearance, we were on our way.

The huge elevator shaft was enough to convince me I wasn't cut out for this kind of story. Called Shaft 2, this was the means of carrying everything from huge trucks to conveyor vehicles down to the mine site. Granted, the trucks had to be partially dismantled, but the pieces were still large enough that they would measure about the same as a sedan car! I was far from over my panic when I gingerly stepped into the enclosed cage, clutching Wally's hand like a drowning man grasping at a shoreline branch, and praying the thing wouldn't stop midway down, leaving us suspended until the next millennium.

Forty-five seconds to a full minute can be an awfully long time when you see your life spinning before your eyes. That's how long it took for the elevator to descend the 1000 feet to the mine level. It felt like an hour.

We stepped out into a scene you might see forty years later in a Stephen Spielberg movie. The entire mine was white: pillars holding the mine solid, the ceiling, walls, floors—all solid white, salt and stone. It was a moderate temperature, and the entire working area had fresh air circulating, which eased my mind considerably.

Huge trucks drove as if they were on a busy street 1000 feet above us. A cafeteria fed the work crews, and every step of the mining operation was constantly monitored. It was easy to see why this operation had succeeded in being accident-free for so long.

I would like to say I was completely comfortable being underground for most of a day. I can't. Paramount on my mind was getting out of there without breaking the company's safety record and getting back up that 1000-foot shaft.

Again, Alan was right. It was a terrific story and we were able to give thousands of people a peek inside a salt mine, because the piece aired coast to coast. I was learning a lot from Alan Maitland.

Hitting My Stride

Windsor at that time was a small enough city that someone with a high profile, such as a commentator for the Mother Network, was soon a figure to be reckoned with. I was called to join organizations I had never heard of, asked to give speeches, attend teas, open church bazaars and commentate fashion shows.

Lazare's Furs was one of the most prominent businesses in the downtown core. Mr. Lazare, a community-minded man with a sound business head, called one day to invite me to his store. I can remember little about the operation, other than here was a family man who obviously adored his daughter. Lining the complete store, hanging from just about every square inch of wall space, were large, framed pictures of this beautiful young woman, taken a year apart from the day she could walk, until she had reached her late teens. I was impressed.

I was there to consider an offer. Mr. Lazare would make available to me, without charge, a fur piece to be worn wherever I went to make a public appearance. The closest I had ever been to a genuine piece of fur was a time, as a young child, when a friend of my mother's came to our farm wearing a set of marten furs around her neck. I remember each little animal had its teeth imbedded into the rear end of the next fur to create a circle. I thought it was just about the most stylish piece of clothing I had ever clapped eyes on. And here I was being offered a fur piece every time I made a public appearance!

Thereafter, the delivery truck would arrive at my door, drop off a coat or stole (stoles were big back then), and off I would go feeling like Mrs. Astor's horse. When the event was over, the truck would dutifully pick up the fur and return it to Lazare's. Mr. Lazare made no demands on me as to advertising the fact that the furs were from his shop. Had he done so, I'm sure Alan Maitland would have quashed the deal before it got off the ground.

Fashion shows were a big item at that time. All were held to benefit a good cause, and it was made clear to me by Alan that reaching out into the community by participating in these shows was not only an obligation on my part, it was a privilege to be asked. It was another way, too, of building a listening audience. I was learning.

In a few short months, we were making inroads into the Detroit listening area. That meant that my community involvement was greatly expanded. I soon found myself running back and forth across the river, meeting commitments which ran the gamut from social engagements to charity work, commercial obligations and generally a repeat of what I was doing in the Windsor district. My workload was tremendous, but the satisfaction I was getting from the job far outweighed the exhaustion I felt at the end of a day.

Happily, there was a never-ending supply of interesting people and events that kept my program agenda full, and so we never had to worry over where we might find the next story.

The word "networking" had yet to be used commonly, but that, in fact, was what we did in order to keep interest high, cover a wide range of topics and bring fascinating people to our listening audience. Those dreaded letters from foreign correspondents still had to be read weekly, but when I complained about their being boring and unimaginative, I was told in no uncertain terms that they would continue to be a part of my programming. I can admit now, so many years later, that I often chopped a few lines out of them. And every time I read one, I prayed I was correct in my pronunciation of names and places I had never heard of, and which I strongly suspected our listeners hadn't either. I don't remember ever being taken to task for making an error in reading these letters, but then again, it may have been that people simply tuned me out at that time in the program.

If I brought a particular talent to broadcasting, it was that I had an insatiable curiosity about people and my surroundings, which I think more than made up for any lack of experience or formal education. I could find stories where none seemed to exist.

A visit to observe someone buying a hat in the accessory department of Hudson's in Detroit was one of the most fun programs I came up with. Finding someone who would let me talk to her on microphone while she made her choice was simple. The customer was delighted to be on radio, and as we worked our way through dozens of hat choices, we soon had an audience around us who were offering advice, entering into the spirit of the program, and creating lots of background sounds which greatly enhanced the story. It turned out to be an hilarious piece, and from that one idea came many others where we used ordinary people doing ordinary things.

We once went through people's garbage on the curb to see what they had discarded.

To help her lose weight, we hypnotized our studio's records librarian.

We followed the same hypnotist to a local fair, a salesmen's pep rally, and to a police station where he helped officers solve a series of petty crimes.

Since Essex County is rich with produce factories and productive farmland, we capitalized on this fact. However, we bypassed the factory and went right into a farm kitchen and taped a housewife pickling and preserving. We sent out hundreds of her recipes to the listening audience who simply had to write in their request.

To keep a balance, of course, we still programmed strikes (which were plentiful in blue-collar Windsor), dealt with industry expansion, and profiled the many artists and cultural events in artistically enriched communities in both Windsor and Detroit.

On the home front, the Cook household was a busy one. Our son was trying to stand, my father-in-law kept an eye on things when I was running the roads, and Wally was in a demanding job. However, a series of events came into play shortly that would turn my life upside down, and cause such an upheaval in our lives that, at the time, I doubted we would ever recover.

Mary and Wally on their wedding day

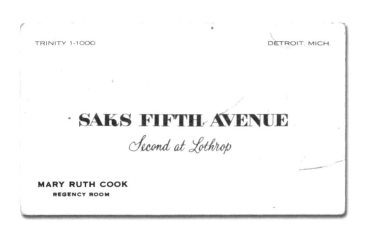

TRINITY 1-1000

DETROIT. MICH.

· SAKS FIFTH AVENUE .

Second at Lothrop

MARY RUTH COOK
REGENCY ROOM

Mary's calling card from Saks Fifth Avenue

Commentating a
fashion show, 1958

Mary's first CBC
publicity shot

Transitions

Going Home

It doesn't matter now what the strike was about. But with little warning, the hundreds of staff at the largest department store in Windsor, where Wally was a divisional manager, hit the picket lines. The strike was a blow to my husband, who prided himself on an honest day's work, and who treated his staff with respect and the utmost consideration.

The walkout came at a very bad time. Windsor was heading into a recession, and the economy was faltering. To add to the problem of the loss of business for the store, thousands of dollars' worth of Easter candy had arrived and was sitting on the shelves awaiting the seasonal business. Wally's requests to remove the candy and donate it to charity were turned down. Although management was allowed in the store, they could do nothing to keep the place open. I watched as Wally grew more despondent with each day the sales staff walked the picket lines.

Out of nowhere came a call from a long-time friend in my

hometown of Carleton Place. Harvey Asselstine owned the Rexall Drug Store, and he was calling to tell us the store Wally had once managed in the main business core was closing. Harvey thought the building, soon to be vacant, would provide us with an ideal opportunity to open our own department store in a community where we were well known.

In retrospect, what we did was rash. We decided to go for it. It was a rash move because we suffered from a severe lack of operating capital, I had just signed a 13-month contract with the CBC, our chances of selling our house in depressed Windsor were just about nil, and we had the well-being of both an infant and an aged parent to consider.

Nevertheless, within days, Wally was on his way back to the Ottawa Valley, and I was left to work out my contract and try to get rid of our house. It was the longest year of my life. It was hard to keep a high interest in my broadcasts while I fretted about the huge undertaking to which we had just committed ourselves, but giving my all to my work had to remain my priority. Alan Maitland was a saint. While he gently made it clear I still had an obligation to the CBC and my listeners, Alan and wife Connie filled the void in my life left by Wally's absence.

I missed my husband terribly. But, also, in the back of my mind was the realization that within the year I would have to give up a job I loved, move from a city that had become home, and leave cherished new friends behind, all the while heading to an uncertain future.

On a day that threatened snow, I flew to Ottawa and then travelled on to Carleton Place to witness the opening of our own business, which I was sure was doomed for failure. Empty boxes filled the shelves to make it look as if we were loaded with stock, dozens of roses were on hand to give out to each customer who entered the door, and Wally was filled with hope. I was filled with despair—especially when the worst blizzard of the century, in my estimation, hit the town and you could barely see the building across the street. The few faithful who braved the blizzard went home with a rose, and at the end of the day, if I remember correctly, we still had most of them on hand.

I flew back to Windsor with mixed emotions. If the store failed, I would still be able to stay in Windsor and keep the job I loved. But it would be a heartbreak to my husband who had worked so hard to open this business.

Although it was a struggle, the store survived that year...and for 38 years thereafter. Wally grew Cook's of Carleton Place from a small operation to one of the most successful junior department stores in the Ottawa Valley.

At the end of that first year, after keeping up the hectic pace at the CBC and with the added burden of keeping things on an even keel on the home front, our house miraculously sold. Despite that relief, my last day at CBE Windsor was one of great sadness, as I was sure my career as a broadcaster was over. Packing my tape recorder, microphone, dozens of files of past broadcasts and letters of good wishes from listeners, I headed home, following the moving van. Pessimistically, I was convinced I would never hold another microphone in my hand, nor chase down an interview, nor feel the rush of adrenalin before a producer signalled a countdown. I was sure my career as a broadcaster was over.

Just a Respite

Within the span of a few years, our family grew to include two more chosen children and my mother, Mabel Haneman. A severe diabetic, Mother had come to live with us after losing a leg. This put four distinct age groups under our roof: Wally's father, now in his late eighties, my mother in her seventies, Wally and I in our forties, and three young children. Our 22-room house throbbed with activity. For a time, picking up a microphone was the farthest thing from my mind.

But I never lost my love of writing, and a chance meeting with an editor of one of Ottawa's daily newspapers, *The Citizen*, wetted my appetite again to get back into journalism. Fred Inglis wondered if I would consider covering the local scene. At his urging, I agreed to try to cram the job of reporting rural news into my already busy life, which included of course, long hours at our growing retail business.

It was easy to reconnect with the community I had left a few years earlier. And once again, it seemed I had more stories to write about than *The Citizen* had room to put into print.

Although it was not exactly the Mother Network, I was also asked to do regular broadcasts from a flourishing private radio station in the neighbouring town of Smiths Falls. CJET gave me a venue for personal opinion, and kept me in touch with broadcasting, which I realized I missed more than I was ready to admit, even though on many occasions, I was a guest on various radio and television shows out of the nation's capital. And so, once again, I was being heard and read by a large audience who seemed to like the homey, yet newsy, stuff I was putting out.

It didn't take long for the CBC to contact me and offer me a freelance position with their Ottawa radio station, CBO. I think now, I was approached for a couple reasons. I had experience. I was known to a wide and diversified audience, and I was as familiar with Ottawa and the Ottawa Valley as a map maker. Starting out with a small role in the station's programming suited me just fine. I did not aspire to being the main voice on a daily show.

In the early 1970s, the CBC seemed to change producers as often as I changed socks. And it was a young energetic guy by the name of Gary Dwyer Joyce who appeared as the producer of "Radio Noon." It was Gary who talked me into increasing my contribution. He liked the folksy items I was doing, and was delighted with the tremendous response we got from listeners when I introduced them to unique Ottawa Valley people, all with a story to tell, adding a warmth and charm to a program that was basically geared to an urban audience. I was moved up to a definite time slot, every Tuesday and Thursday, in the second hour of the two-hour show.

Rarely did I have the use of a technician. So investing in the best taping equipment I could buy, I took on this new challenge. It was expected that I would cover a wide geographic area. In fact, my stories of people, places and topics came from as far away as Belleville on the southwest, to Algonquin Park on the extreme northwest, right through to the Quebec border on the east, and across the Ottawa River into Western Quebec. It was a vast area to cover, and once again I was faced with the dilemma of choosing the best pieces for the show, while passing up others because of the lack of air time. It was a good dilemma to be faced with.

CBC in Ottawa was a heavily listened-to station. "Radio Noon" drew a large listening audience from all walks of life—both urban and rural. The people I interviewed gave their stories so willingly, and that, perhaps more than any expertise on my part, allowed me the honour of receiving several ACTRA awards for excellence in broadcasting. By the time Gary Dwyer Joyce moved on and a new producer took over his desk, my segment of the show was well established, and once again, I was in demand for everything from fashion shows to cooking schools, and from judging dog shows and chili contests to doing readings in rural and urban classrooms.

The young man who subsequently took over as producer for "Radio Noon" was full of innovative ideas. Joe Novak was so enthralled with the simple stories of the rural community and its people, that he asked if I would consider co-hosting the show. The show already had a first-class host, Bill Kehoe, who had been with the network for many years, and I wondered how it would sit with this long-time broadcaster to have an upstart from the country sitting opposite him in Studio H.

Partners

To work closely together, a host and co-host must have a mutual respect for each other. They may not always agree, but working toward a common goal, and achieving the best possible program for the listening audience, must always be the most important objective.

There is no room for personal agendas and pet peeves. A smoothly running show takes precedent over individual biases. Working as host and co-host is always a joint effort.

The wise words above came to me directly from Alan Maitland. When I was offered the co-host chair for "Radio Noon," I called my mentor for advice. Alan's success working with Barbara Frum on "As It Happens" was no doubt in large part because the advice he gave me was his personal creed. His parting words to me were "go for it."

Bill Kehoe and I had worked together before. We always got

along well. But I was concerned about being his co-host, even for only two days a week. After all, he *was* "Radio Noon."

Bill was a seasoned broadcaster, and he knew the Ottawa Valley as well as I did. Born in Pembroke, Ontario, he came from a long line of respected town fathers. His grandfather and uncles made a name for themselves as superior builders, and the post office and the Public Library in Pembroke were designed by Francis Sullivan, a pupil of Frank Lloyd Wright, and built by the Kehoes. Bill had a high stake in the Ottawa Valley. He was the small town boy who "made good." When he started out in broadcasting, he was first with CHOV in Pembroke, and then headed for Sudbury to CKSOT, the first privately owned television station in Canada.

While on a holiday back in Eastern Ontario, he accepted an on-air spot with CFRA, owned by Frank Ryan, ironically, the man who first put a microphone in my hand at the country fairs. He was then lured to television by the manager of CJOH in Ottawa, and finally ended up at the CBC. He was to stay with the network for 31 years, never without a daily show.

And so it was with more than a little apprehension that I first sat across the table from Bill Kehoe as his co-host. I knew he was a professional. I knew he was a stickler for accuracy, and I knew he had his own opinion about how "Radio Noon" should come across to the listener.

Bill also had one of the sharpest minds in radio. He had a photographic memory, and could recall names, dates and places most of us had long ago put out of our minds. He had a healthy sense of humour, but could be deadly serious when it came to programming.

It was obvious to everyone that it would be physically impossible for me to cover my wide territory and be in the studio five days a

Mary Cook • 58

week. And so it was decided, with Bill Kehoe's blessing, that I would share the host duties two days a week. The rest of the time I would be running the highways and side roads of Eastern Ontario, doing what I did best: meeting people, searching out off-beat places and stories, and occasionally dipping into the hard news items introduced to me by Alan Maitland back in Windsor.

Although only in the studio two days a week, involvement with the show was turning into a seven-day-a-week job. I had to come up with three pieces for each Tuesday and Thursday. With such a vast area from which to search out the items, it meant putting on as much as six or seven hundred miles a week on my car. My tape recorder went everywhere with me, even to church on Sunday. Stories turned up in the most unusual places, and a wide network of contacts continually supplied me with suggestions for the show.

At the outset I ran willy-nilly from one end of my listening audience to the other, chasing interviews. And then I learned the hard way that I was wasting valuable time, spending travelling money unnecessarily, and wearing myself out criss-crossing the Ottawa Valley, sometimes for only one short interview. I felt there had to be a better way of covering the area without backtracking hundreds of miles and coming home with only one story. I began setting up appointments and using my contacts to tie down several interviews in one trip. For instance, if a story took me to the city of Cornwall on the extreme east of my territory, I contacted several key people along the road to Cornwall. I inquired about people who had interesting stories to tell in their area, called those individuals suggested to me (most of whom were more than willing to share their experiences), and usually ended up with eight to ten interviews ahead of me—all to be taped on the one trip.

So that the items would be as diversified as possible, and not all from the one area, I had the luxury of mixing up the stories, because I always had at least a dozen "in the can" ahead of me. Some of them would be short and newsy, and some would be filled with human interest.

Although we didn't always agree on every item I put in the lineup, Bill and I worked around our differences, and with very few exceptions, I think now on looking back, "Radio Noon" was always a great show when we worked together. The human interest touch I was able to bring to the program gained momentum quickly, and the team of Bill Kehoe and Mary Cook, although I was only in the studio two days a week, was soon an accepted part of CBO radio.

Back in stride, I was once again doing what I loved. The space between working with the CBC in Windsor and now Ottawa was little more than a respite. The lure of broadcasting was as deep in my soul as my strong belief that I was contributing to a meaningful picture of interesting people and places. I knew their stories were not being reported. Although I was told many times that what I was doing was unique in Canada, I'm not at all sure that was a fact. There may have been other broadcasters in the country who were going out with tape recorders in hand, and bringing back to the studio the same kind of stories I was finding. What I do know is that I was being allowed into the very hearts of ordinary people, many whom were leading extraordinary lives, and who were trusting me to tell their stories with honesty and integrity. It was my challenge to take those stories and make them come alive. It was a challenge I would meet every day for the next 22 years.

Studio Days

 It would be impossible to profile all the people with whom I came in contact while working out of the studio located on the seventh floor of the famous Château Laurier in Ottawa, long-time home to CBC radio. As I said, producers came and went as if they were passing through swinging doors. The same was true of the on-air people who filled in for show hosts on a regular basis.

Bob Knapp, who had a bass voice that I thought literally bounced off the walls when he was on-air, was a veteran CBC announcer. It was always a delight when Bob filled in on "Radio Noon" or any of the other shows on which I often found myself. We had done some television work together, as well as some special programming that was well received by the listeners. Bob Knapp and Bill Kehoe were long-time friends. They bounced humour off each other when they happened to be on the same show, and generally let the listener know they were enjoying every on-air minute. Bob Knapp read the news, and I can remember one time when I thought their practical joking was going to cost us our jobs.

Bob Knapp was right in the middle of a serious news item when Bill reached over, flicked on his lighter and lit the corner of Bob's script. Bob tried to silently squelch the blaze, keep the rest of his script from going up in flames, and still maintain the sense of decorum expected of all CBC personnel. I cringed in a corner, waiting for the station master to come rushing in with a bucket of water. At the very least, I feared we would start the fire alarms clanging in the halls. How Bob managed to finish reading the news without losing his place in the script, or keep the entire felt-covered table from erupting into a three-alarm fire, remains a mystery to me to this day!

Back then, broadcasting was fun. Although everyone took their job seriously, there was always an undercurrent of merriment, enhanced further by the sheer love of the job. Often that fun was transmitted to the listeners, who on many occasions let us know through phone calls and mail that they laughed right along with us.

I recall the time Bill Kehoe and I got into the giggles over some story we were doing about chickens. I no longer remember what the story was about. I can only remember convulsive laughter on both our parts, and wondering how we were going to continue. I also remember one listener who phoned immediately after we closed the show that day to tell us she had no idea what we were laughing at, but that she was doubled over, too. Calls like that convinced us that although "Radio Noon" dealt with many serious topics, we had to bring a sense of fun to the program, as well.

In those days, listeners had no trouble reaching the on-air personalities. They simply phoned the station and asked for the person they wanted to speak to, and if it was you, you took the call. We also had our names in the phone book. I don't know of anyone in the 1970s, '80s and early '90s who couldn't be reached by simply dialing the number listed in the local telephone book. Sadly, that has all changed. For security reasons, most on-air performers have unlisted numbers today.

Also, in those glory days, people wandered in off the street at will. They could come up to the seventh floor and visit the studio, meet the performers, and generally move about freely. That, too, has had to change. Now, tight security prevents anyone from going beyond the vestibule after getting off the elevator, and even the "regulars" have entry cards to open the locked doors.

• • •

My story would not be complete without introducing you to a producer who greatly impacted my life in radio, and was responsible for my branching out into another area that would introduce me to thousands of people all over the world. Shirley Gobeil was someone I liked after our first "hello." Shirley blew into the studio every day like a whirling helicopter rotor blade. Everyone knew the instant she arrived. She never just walked anywhere, she stomped down the hall with her arms full of papers, both shoulders holding up tote bags, briefcase and purse. One look told you she meant business.

Shirley and I have different versions of how we got to work together. If you meet her, you can listen to her story. This is mine.

She was producer of the Saturday morning show called "In Town and Out." It was a three-hour program filled with local interest stories and highlights of upcoming events around the nation's capital and the Ottawa Valley. It was a tightly packed format, and Shirley strove to bring a freshness to each show. As I remember it, one of her planned interviews failed to appear, and in a moment of near panic that happens when a producer is faced with dead air time, Shirley asked me if I would put together a story based on a memory of my life on the farm as a young child during the Depression.

I came up with about six minutes of a recollection as told through the eyes of a seven-year-old girl. Time has erased what the story was about; I only remember that it was aired in 1976. Once the item was over, I recall the telephone lighting up like a Christmas tree, as listeners wondered if there would be more "memory" stories on future broadcasts. Shirley Gobeil, with an eye and ear tuned to listener reaction, asked me to write another one for the following week.

What started out as a one-shot deal, turned into a 27-year venture for me, and opened up another opportunity to broaden my scope as a broadcaster. The stories were an instant success. Only a producer as astute as Shirley Gobeil could know how well received those pieces would be and take a chance on branching into another type of programming on a show that had long-established itself as an information vehicle.

Using real people in the happenings I remembered as a child, these pieces became known as the "thirties" stories. And although I never expected them to go much beyond my once-a-week contribution to "In Town and Out," they would grow in popularity and put me smack dab back into the of business of writing. Adding this to two studio days and three-plus days on the road made for a crammed agenda, full of excitement, new experiences and coping with deadlines which forever loomed before me like someone holding a hatchet above my head. I loved every minute of it.

Innovation in Programming

When I was given the opportunity of co-hosting "Radio Noon" in Ottawa, I came into the job with a million ideas. There was no doubt that reaching out beyond the city limits would always remain a top priority in programming. But I was blessed with producers who were open to new ideas that would not only keep the rural interest strong, but further develop the large urban audience, as well.

Some of the ideas I brought to the table, I admit now, were off the wall. Making toffee on snow in Major's Hill Park behind the Château Laurier, when the drifts were waist-deep and we had to lug equipment, notepads and ourselves, sounded like a good idea at the time. It ended up with us panting for breath as we hit the air seconds before the clock. My host and I were hysterical from laughing, and we almost perished in the bargain. When we met for the story meeting afterwards, we listened to phone calls from listeners who had loved every minute of it. However, we vowed in the future that while we would still bring a sense of fun to the show, we would pick stories and places that were a little more compatible with radio.

One year, I thought it would be a good idea to bring to our listeners a well-thought-out plan to take the hassle out of Christmas. I suggested we, first of all, offer suggestions on how to save money during the holiday season. And then I would work out a weekly plan, with a point-by-point strategy, to head into Christmas day with nothing more to do than watch the turkey cooking in the oven while you sat with your family around you, drank hot mulled cider and opened Christmas presents.

We would include a full Christmas menu with step-by-step instructions, so that when the big day rolled around, all you had to do was stuff the bird and relax. The entire meal would be in the freezer. This idea came about when my producer and I were talking about taking Christmas pictures, and I lamented that I was never in any of our family's Christmas photos because I was always in the kitchen peeling turnips. That is until the year I decided something had to change, and I embarked on a plan that I called simply, "taking the hassle out of Christmas."

None of us dreamed the plan would take off as it did. It took months of planning on my part, all the while still having to come up with my regular programming. During the first couple of weeks, we presented ideas on making shopping easier, cheaper and more fun. And by the time we were ready to roll with the recipe handouts, our audience was hooked.

We thought we might mail out perhaps 100 copies of the recipes, but by the time we were nearing the last week before Christmas, we had mailed out more then 3000 packets! We figured that menu would be on the tables of just about everyone in

Ottawa, as we encouraged our listeners to share their copies to cut down on CBC's mail-out costs. It was an idea that surpassed our fondest dreams, and along the way we know we attracted many listeners to "Radio Noon," proving once again that it was the down-home, simple shows that attracted an audience.

Radio listeners love stories about children. I thought we should include a series in our Christmas programming on children in the rural areas. My producer was dubious. After all, children can be unpredictable. But I thought that would be the charm of the whole idea.

I headed out with my tape recorder to a kindergarten class in a public school in the Ottawa Valley town of Almonte. The class was getting ready for a Christmas concert. The teacher hadn't told the youngsters they were to have a visitor. As soon as they saw the microphone, of course, they all wanted to be heard. I decided to 'scan,' so they all thought they were going to be part of the broadcast. There were no inhibitions, no holding back. I just let the tape roll. I taped about an hour of chatter, interruptions, giggles and profound comments. Here are a few:

"I am never going to be in another Christmas concert. I am always a sheep, and next time I am going to be an angel or I'm just not going to play."

"Jamie can't be in the play, because he hit Kelly with the horn. He was only supposed to hold it, but he just swung it around on purpose and Kelly fell right across his desk. So Miss Cuthbert said he would have to behave or he was not going to be in the play. I don't think he should be in it anyway because he doesn't even believe in Santa Claus."

"Do you know we may not be going to have turkey this Christmas? We had it last year and Daddy threw up. He said it was the turkey, but Mommy said it was because he was too long at the Legion."

I wanted to know what their daddies did to help with the Christmas preparations. One little guy took on a look of deep concentration, and then said, "Oohhh, my Daddy just sleeps around."

Little Harry said that Mommy didn't let Daddy help anymore, because he always burned the potatoes and spilt the gravy. "Mommy said he does it on purpose."

And then apropos to absolutely nothing, one little girl with long blonde braids actually grabbed the microphone out of my hand and said, "We speak Hunkgaryink in our house. We don't speak English. And besides, my sister has scratch marks all over her stomach from playing in the cat litter box."

And again leading nowhere, a young boy of about five announced that his father had just won the big lottery. Both the teacher and I looked at him in amazement which he immediately took as doubt on our parts, so he added, "It was an awful lot of money. He had to go all the way to Montreal to get it. And there was so much money, he had to bring it home in a paper bag."

The teacher was so thrilled for the parent that she phoned to congratulate him that night. Immediately thereafter, the father called me, begging me to cut that part out of the interview. "I have no idea where he got that bit of news. I have never bought a lottery ticket in my life." Too bad; it would have made a good clip in the tape.

Before packing up my equipment, I let those who wanted to, hold the microphone. One little girl looked it over, ran her fingers over the big CBC logo and then asked, "Is this going to go on CFRA?" (A local radio competitor.) My producer decided to leave that last comment on the tape for broadcast.

It takes hours to edit a tape of children. There are many pauses,

and what we call ins and outs, but those interviews in kindergarten classrooms at Christmas became a tradition on "Radio
Noon." We always had tremendous response from them, proving
once again that it isn't only interviews with the country's movers
and shakers that can stir the heart of a radio audience.

Above: One of the judges at a local event, I am fourth from the left.

Left: Bill Kehoe, host of "Radio Noon"

Below: Cooking up Christmas menus in Studio H

Clockwise from top left:
Connie Maitland,
Wally, Al Maitland,
me, Jim Cameron

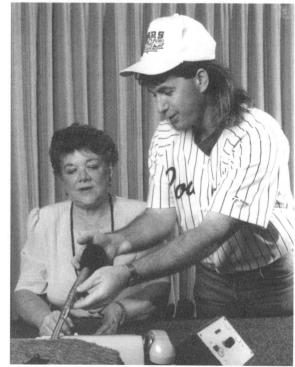

I was always blessed
with the best
technicians in the
business.

Storytelling at local schools

Burning Rubber

And Miles to Go...

Covering a wide territory gave me a mammoth scope for story possibilities. Getting ready for the almost daily trips over the field, meant delegating work on the home front, and depending on the co-operation of my husband. Knowing how much I loved my job, Wally did everything humanly possible to make things run smoothly when I was on the road. Since much of my travelling meant driving over roads that were sometimes barely passable, Wally made sure my car was in top condition and always full of gas. Although I tried always to be home for dinner at night, often I was caught miles from home and had to spend the night in some small hotel in a remote part of my wide territory. Both the children and Wally realized that this was the price we all had to pay for me to do my job.

Anyone who hasn't done the kind of programming I was doing would understandably assume it was simply a case of running around gathering stories and then going back to the station and rolling the tapes. Oh, if that were only the case! The reality was much different.

After setting up the appointments in a given territory, it became a race against time to make sure these appointments were met on schedule. I was dealing with busy people for the most part—people who were going out of their way and giving up their time to talk to me on tape. I prided myself on being punctual, and this meant trying to pace the road time and the actual interview, so that the space I had allotted for that particular story didn't run hopelessly over, making *me* hopelessly late for the next stop! It wasn't always easy, but for the most part I was able to stay close to schedule.

With any luck, I would come home with at least a half dozen stories taped. To get them, I may have put a few hundred miles or more on the car, but I would have come home with two or three 60-minute cassettes full.

Then the true grunt work began. Those tapes would have to be brought to the radio station and dubbed to a reel, so that I could bring them home to be edited. Remember, this was all new territory for me. I had never edited tape before. It meant buying an expensive machine, learning how to stop and start it at exactly the right spot, cut and splice, and most importantly, learn what to take out and what to leave in. And always, I had to remember not to throw any scraps of tape into the waste basket until I was sure I had saved what was important.

The interview may have run up to two hours. It was my challenge to cut that interview down to a workable size. That could mean anywhere from five to twenty minutes, depending on the story. Today, technicians would do this all by computer. When I was doing my own editing, I would spend hours hunched over the editing machine to come up with those few minutes. There was scarcely a night I got to bed before midnight. Depending on the interview, it could take up to six hours to edit one story. But, of course, editing wasn't the end of the process.

Making notes while I edited, I then had to script the piece, which meant I had to come up with dialogue for Bill Kehoe and me to read during the airing of the interview. It had to be perfectly timed; being out by as little as two seconds could mean disaster in the studio when the program aired.

Getting the piece by the producer, and convincing him or her that the item merited the time I allotted for it, was another challenge. Rarely did the producer accept the item without cutting a few seconds out here and a minute out there. It was frustrating, but you didn't argue with the producer! And they were invariably right. It was their job to work many pieces into the time allotted to the entire show, and I often thought what I did was far less stressful than their job of compacting a show of varied items into a fixed time slot.

Having said that, I have always thought I could get along without a producer, but I could never get along without a good technician. A technician will make or break a broadcaster. He will know how to push the right buttons to modulate your voice. He will cover for you when you err, and will be there to roll a cut of music when you falter. I was blessed with the best technicians in the business. There is no doubt in my mind that these guys (I think I only had one female technician all the time I was in the Ottawa studio) played a very big role in whatever success I enjoyed as a broadcaster.

I have always said, too, that I travelled the roads with an angel on my shoulder, because I seemed to be in the right place at the right time. Just happening on a good story by chance became more than a coincidence, and with very few exceptions, my choices of interviews worked out to have great listener appeal. I am convinced this was not always the result of my expertise, but rather because someone or something was directing me.

War Nurse

It should have been one of those run of the mill, ordinary interviews. It turned out to be a fascinating story of intrigue, adventure and clandestine manoeuvring, such as I had never been involved with in radio.

We wanted to do a story on an old-time war nurse for our Remembrance Day show. After numerous enquiries, we finally came up with the name Evelyn Pepper.

I sat in Evelyn's comfortable bungalow in the west end of Ottawa while she told me about enlisting in 1940 and ending up in Italy at the front lines with her nursing unit. She talked about the inadequate facilities and how the army doctors worked around the clock trying to keep up with the steady stream of injured being brought in on stretchers. It was turning into a wonderful human interest interview I knew my listeners would love.

And then her story took a twist. She remarked that one of the most gratifying moments at the front line in that makeshift hospital came when she was able to talk a 17-year-old Canadian soldier into having surgery to save his shattered arm. Barely more than a boy, he had been badly wounded. The doctor knew he had to operate, but the terrified young soldier refused to allow the doctor to touch him. In desperation, the army doctor went to Evelyn and told her he didn't care how she did it, but she had to convince the soldier to let him do what he had to do. He also told Evelyn that not only would the young lad lose his arm if he wasn't tended to immediately, he would probably lose his life, as well.

Evelyn talked to the soldier, but he stuck to his guns. He wasn't going to let any doctor operate out there in a tent, with bullets flying overhead, and that's all there was to it. Evelyn began to formulate a plan. First, she gained the confidence of the soldier, and then she challenged him to a bet. "I'll make a deal with you. If I can guess where you were born, within a 30-mile radius, you will have the operation. If I'm wrong, we'll forget about it and you will just have to accept the consequences." The young soldier considered the odds, and figured there was no way this nurse, in the front lines in Italy, was going to guess where he was born. Thinking he couldn't lose, he agreed to the bet.

The young soldier didn't count on just how cagey that nurse was!

Evelyn was well acquainted with the Ottawa Valley, and was pretty sure she recognized a deep Renfrew County accent. "You were born close to the town of Renfrew in the Ottawa Valley," she said, as her heart raced and she prayed she was right.

The flabbergasted soldier admitted he was born in Renfrew County. He was caught. He came from hardy rural stock, where honesty was your bond, and a deal was a deal. He had lost the bet, fair and square, and Evelyn Pepper began to prep him for surgery.

As she told me the story, an idea began to form in my mind. I asked her if she remembered his name. She thought it might be Jeffrey, but she wasn't sure if that was his last or first name. "It was so long ago," she said. "I can remember how terrified he was, and how I held his good hand all the time the doctor was operating."

And then I did something a good broadcaster should never do. I told a barefaced lie to the interviewee, as a plan began to form in my mind.

I said the story of her war experiences would be so much better if they were told "live" on air, and we would just forget about the taped interview. Evelyn Pepper was a very private person, and she hesitated at the thought of being live in the studio. I had to do some sweet-talking, and she reluctantly agreed to come to the Château Laurier for the interview, so that it could be broadcast on Remembrance Day.

I made no mention of the boy soldier. But as soon as I left her home, I set to work.

How do you find a soldier who was by then probably in his late sixties, whose name you did not know, and all you really knew about him was that he was born in Renfrew County and had suffered a serious arm injury during the Second World War? Renfrew County was one of the largest counties in the province of Ontario; Remembrance Day was three weeks away. Not a lot of time to sleuth for an unknown.

Through a network of wonderful Renfrew County people, including John Patrick Grogan, himself a boy soldier, and local historians Len and Irene Quilty, we were able to learn that a young lad with the last name of Jeffrey had indeed served in Italy as a young soldier and had suffered a serious arm injury. But, alas, he lived in

Elliott Lake. They thought... Nobody knew for sure. No one was certain he was even still alive. Finding this veteran began to look like an impossible mission.

And so the long distance calls began. Dozens of false leads and fruitless calls later, I still hadn't made a connection. And Remembrance Day was looming closer and closer.

I had all but given up, when I connected with someone by the name of Gerald Jeffery in Elliott Lake. Yes, he had been in the Second World War. And yes, he had suffered a serious arm wound in Italy. I tried to explain why I was calling, but at the outset, he was very reluctant to talk to me. And certainly, he didn't want to dwell on his days as a young soldier in Italy!

And then I told him about the nurse who had saved his life, and our plan to bring her into the studio for our Remembrance Day broadcast. I wondered if he would come to Ottawa and appear while she was telling her story, but of course, the whole exercise would be a surprise to her. He finally agreed, and arrangements were made to bring him to Ottawa on the very day I had invited Evelyn Pepper to the studio for her interview.

The entire seventh floor of the Château Laurier was buzzing that day. Everyone knew what was happening, and no one knew how the interview would turn out, or if the whole scheme would blow up in my face.

It was my job to get her around to talking about the boy with the injured arm. No small feat when you consider that Evelyn Pepper thought she was there to talk about the generalities of serving as a nurse during the war. We skirted the issue for many minutes. Finally, I was able to steer her in the direction of the story, and she told about her experience and how she had conned him into the surgery.

I asked her if she knew what had happened to the young soldier. "No, I'm afraid not. In fact, he may even have died later. I have no way of knowing. I don't even remember his name."

And at that very moment, my producer walked Gerald Jeffrey through the studio door. The war veteran bared his arm to Evelyn, and asked, "Does this look like the arm you helped save?"

I don't have to tell you that even my six-foot-tall technician was crying, as was everyone else in the control room. The interview disintegrated before my eyes, as Evelyn Pepper, this wonderful war nurse, and the once-young Canadian soldier embraced and sobbed. We ended up running war songs for the rest of the show, because no one in the studio could say a word without crying.

We were flooded with calls and letters over that interview, and I don't think any piece ever gave me such joy and satisfaction during my long tenure with the CBC. Evelyn Pepper is dead now, but she lived long enough to receive the Order of Canada.

Mrs. Sullivan and Her Boys

In this business you soon learn not to pass up stories which from the outset might not appear to be front-page news. Because you never know what kind of sleeper is hiding underneath the surface.

This was the case on one day when I was in the small Western Quebec village of Chapeau. The entire community seemed to stretch along a very short street that also served as the main highway. I didn't expect to get much more than the story I had come for, which was an interview with a gentleman who had had a long career in amateur boxing. Recently moved to Chapeau, he had started a training program for some of the young boys from the area.

It was an interesting interview, but not earth-shattering. I asked the question I always asked when visiting a new community, and when I was about to pack up my tape recorder and head for home.

"Are there any interesting people here who may have an unusual story to tell?" My interviewee didn't miss a beat when he asked, "Can you spare a few minutes? If so, I'd like you to meet someone who has lived in this community all her life, and I think you might be interested in her story."

It was a wild day. Rain had turned to sleet, and the highway, which I could see from his front window, was fast turning to an ice bed. But I didn't want to take a chance on missing a good story. We headed out, bundled against the elements. Slipping and sliding down a hill, he directed me to turn into a road that seemed to lead into a dense bush.

Sitting in a grove was a two-storey house, its wood now almost black from years without the benefit of a coat of paint. The yard was as neat as a pin, but it was obvious that whoever lived in this home, did so in abject poverty. It was hard to imagine that this particular setting might be home to a good story.

The woman who met us at the door was small, and I immediately assessed that she was much younger than she appeared. Her handshake was warm and welcoming, and she steered us into a sparsely furnished kitchen that was as neat as the outside yard.

The man who had taken me there said he felt her life would be of interest to my listeners. Here is her story:

Ethel Sullivan's claim to fame was that she had been married 21 years when she had 19 children. And they were all boys!

Ethel knew what poverty meant. If it hadn't been for the Catholic Church, she doubted she could have survived. It kept her boys clothed so that they could go to school, but sometimes there was only enough money to buy five or six pairs of shoes. When that was the case, those boys who got the footwear were the only ones who started out for the village school in the morning.

Every day, Ethel cooked an enormous pot of porridge. This was their breakfast. What was left over from the previous day was chilled out in the summer kitchen, sliced and put between two slices of bread for school lunches.

Supper that night saw Ethel fry the rest of the porridge in pork fat. To that she added vegetables she had grown on her patch of land, and their bellies were almost satisfied until the next day.

She told me that sometimes, when she was desperate, she would send her older boys out into the village to see if the "rich people" (as she called those who were better off than she was, although it is doubtful anyone was really "rich" in Chapeau) could spare a bit of food. Rarely did they come home with anything, but Ethel vows it was the "poor" people who were willing to share what they had.

Ethel told me how one day Father Harrington, the parish priest, came to visit and saw Ethel trying to wash clothes on a scrub board placed inside an old tub full of holes. Ethel had tried to plug the holes with bits of rags wrapped around small sticks, but she wasn't too successful in stopping the water from running out on the ground. Father Harrington went away and came back with a new washtub. Since he had stopped at the general store on the way, the tub was filled with groceries.

On one occasion, when her boys were desperately in need of clothes, she prevailed upon the owner of the general store, and he gave her credit with the agreement that she would pay off the bill—at the rate of one dollar each month. She said she never missed a payment.

Ethel talked about how she was the disciplinarian. Her husband worked in the bush, and so the work of running the house and looking after her large family of boys was left entirely in her hands. And she believed in prayer. No one went to bed at night without kneeling for prayers around Ethel's knees. And they went to church, no excuses. The church was good to them, and they would reciprocate by being regular attendees.

When I talked with one son, Ned, who still lives in Chapeau, he said he never recalled going to bed hungry. The food was far from plentiful, but he said there was always enough to eat, mainly because his mother was so frugal and such a good manager. Each of the babies had been born at home. The older boys were expected to look after the younger ones. Sleeping arrangements were simple. Four or five to a bed, and often crossways. Ned remembered how when the boys were upstairs getting ready for bed, he could hear his mother moving around downstairs, cooking, mending, washing and getting ready for the next day. Of course, there was no electricity, phone, plumbing or refrigeration.

When the Second World War came, only one boy was old enough to go overseas. Ethel spent many hours with her rosary, praying for William's safe return. Someone gave her an old battery-powered radio, and Ned remembers her sitting at night listening to the war news and crying softly. When Bill, as the brothers called him, came home, he was awarded the Military Medal for Bravery. Ethel said she was never more proud, especially when she learned that the medal had been presented to her son by the king!

Ethel's garden helped feed her gang of boys, and in the summer time she sent them off to pick berries. They would be gone all day. Ned laughed when he recalled going deep into the bush with the instruction from his mother to keep whistling so they wouldn't get separated from each other. It also prevented them from eating the berries, he said.

And then one day, Ethel's husband was severely injured in a

lumber camp accident. He came home an invalid, and until the day he died, he never worked again.

Today, 12 of the 19 boys remain. Mostly, they have stayed in the Chapeau area, working as trappers, hunters and guides. They grew up to be honest, hard-working people. Ethel is gone now, but she will long be remembered in Western Quebec as the woman who raised 19 children, all of whom happened to be boys.

Alan Maitland once told me every story should open with a bang to keep the listener's interest, and should close the same way so the piece would be remembered. As I was ready to pack up my microphone in Ethel Sullivan's kitchen that day, I was looking for that close that would stay with the listener. I asked Ethel why she had so many children. With a sparkle in her eyes and a wide, knowing smile, she leaned into the microphone and said, "Well, my husband worked in the bush, you know. And once a year he came home to apologize." And then she laughed and laughed, and so did I. When I was editing the piece, I left the laughter right on the tape where I found it. I had the closing that would be remembered.

Pig

Exotic woods. What could that mean? Well, to a person seeking out interesting stories and people, it meant turning off the highway and down a long driveway to find out.

I rapped on the door of a spanking new, board house...crafted perhaps with the same "exotic wood" advertised at the roadside. The man who answered the door wore a rakish cap and tweed jacket with leather elbow patches. He wasn't tall, but he gave the impression of being powerful. Jack Semlar thrust out a hand which I immediately noticed was missing a few fingers. When I told him I was interested in doing a story on his business of importing and selling specialty woods, he graciously invited me into his office at the front of his house, which I noted was panelled with beautiful, honey-coloured wood.

Jack had a heavy European accent, and when he said, "Watch the peeg," I had no idea what he was saying. That is, until I looked in the direction he was pointing, right into the decidedly unfriendly eyes of an enormous black and pink pig. Even my life on the farm as a little girl did little to quell the mounting fear I felt towards this animal that, to me, should have been outside rolling in the mud...and not in Jack Semlar's office!

Jack seemed nonplussed at my apprehension over his house guest, and assured me that Pig was as gentle as a lamb. That was the animal's name. Just plain Pig. Nothing fancy. I soon realized there was a better story here than the one about exotic woods.

While scratching a now-contented Pig behind the ears, Jack told me how he had come to have this farm animal living in his house. It seems he was delivering a load of wood to a farm near Brockville. The farmer had a piggery, and amongst the litter of newborns was one that looked very much like it would never see the light of another day. "It was scrawny, could hardly stand up, and kept getting routed out of its feeding spot on the mother sow," Jack said. The farmer agreed with Jack that it was unlikely this runt of the litter would last much longer.

Jack Semlar asked for and was given the pig, which he brought back with him to his farm and lumberyard just outside of Perth, Ontario. Pig settled in as if she had been born in the kitchen. She took over a spot behind the cookstove, and thrived on whatever it was Jack fed her.

For some reason Jack was never able to explain, he just didn't get around to moving Pig to the barn. She swam in the swimming pool with Jack's two dogs, and generally did whatever they did, which included running the fields and coming back to Jack when they were called. She was growing fast. No longer was Pig the little runt Jack had rescued from almost-certain death. The Landrace pig was now a whopping 274 pounds, with the beautiful pink and black markings of a prized swine.

Jack adored Pig, and Pig obviously adored Jack. The only problem that had developed was Pig's insane jealousy of anyone who came near Jack or intruded on her territory in the house. Thus Pig's look of malice when I entered Jack's office.

It was obvious to me that this was no ordinary pig. She was as smart as a whip, and Jack maintained that pigs are just about the smartest farm animal there is. And as for being dirty? Don't you believe it!

Pig went everywhere with Jack. He had a big red, four-door Cadillac, from which he had removed the back seat. All Jack had to do was rattle the keys and Pig was at the ready. She would climb into the cavity where the back seat had been, sit on her haunches and gaze out at the scenery, as she and Jack went cruising through the countryside. It was one of these excursions that almost cost Jack his license, and caused a minor mishap on the streets of Perth.

Jack had stopped abreast of another car at a traffic light. The woman driving the other vehicle happened to glance out her window...right into the grinning face of Pig. She became so rattled she put her foot to the floor and clipped off a pole at the side of the road. Jack was ordered to keep Pig at home.

That ban didn't come into effect before I had a chance to display Pig at a public function in the nation's capital, however. We were taking our CBC show to one of Ottawa's more elite shopping locations—240 Sparks Street. I thought it would be great fun to have Pig as a special guest.

There was a ban against transporting domestic animals through the City of Ottawa, and we had to get police permission and an escort to carry out our plan. Jack and Pig drove up in style to 240 Sparks Street, and the throngs there to greet them made all the effort worthwhile.

Pig had been prettied up for the occasion. She had had a bath and was glistening like silk. Jack had tied a wide pink ribbon around her neck, and she didn't seem to mind the leash he used to get her into the rotunda of the complex. The maintenance staff had been warned that a pig would be part of the remote broadcast, and they were there with short brooms and dustpans, waiting for what they were sure would be an inevitable mess. They underestimated Pig—she was completely housebroken. When the show was over, there wasn't as much as a straw in evidence to indicate that she had been there.

Everyone loved Pig. They patted her, hugged her, and fed her muffins and donuts. She was in her glory. She performed the few tricks she had learned, including shaking hands with her front leg, and sitting down on her haunches when she was told. Pig was a hit, Jack Semlar was proud, and I was relieved that my gamble for a unique show had paid off.

It was obvious that Pig was out of the ordinary. In many ways. She even learned to open the door at Jack's house by wrapping that big jaw around the doorknob so that she could come and go as she pleased.

Alas, according to Jack, Pig grew into a hopeless alcoholic. And it was all because of her love of fermented apples. Jack had several apple trees in his yard, and for some reason, Pig preferred to eat them in the dead of night rather than in broad daylight.

One fall night, Pig let herself out of the house and filled her belly with the fermented apples that had fallen from the trees and lay rotting on the ground. She must have had a good feed, because it was assumed later that she had eaten enough to get roary-eyed drunk. She wandered out onto Highway 7, lay down in the middle of the road, and an eighteen-wheeler did the rest.

It was the end of Pig. We all mourned the loss of a very special animal, who thought like a human, lived like a queen, figured she was a dog, and possessed the very human emotion of jealousy.

The Actra award I won for the initial interview with Jack Semlar should have gone to Pig, because she was the true star of the program. Years later, people who either heard that first interview or attended the remote broadcast still talk about Pig. They come up to me and say, "Mind the time you had that pig on your show? Whatever became of her?" And with a sadness I never thought I would feel for a pig, I tell the story of a farm animal that earned the right to live in a human environment.

Visiting with bottle collector Shirley Shorter. Shirley's father operated the first private radio station in the national capital, running it from the family dining room.

I regularly hosted listener parties in my 22-room country home. People wrote in and names were drawn. After enjoying a moonlight sleigh ride, the group was ready to tuck into a ham and bean buffet.

Ethel Sullivan and her husband with 13 of her sons. Six were yet to arrive!

Oakley Bush of Alexandria, Ontario, takes me (and my listeners) for a ride in an antique buggy.

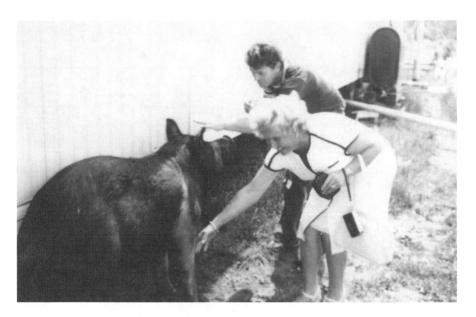

"Pig" gets a visit from some of her "fans"

Older and Wiser

The First Anniversary

What started out as one special item, became a regular weekly feature on "Radio Noon." Deep in the Ottawa Valley one day, I happened on an elderly couple sitting on a bench in a small rural hamlet. It was a hot day and I stopped, more to catch a breath beside the waterfront than to strike up a conversation.

But it's hard, in this part of the world, to come face to face with anyone and not enter into a dialogue. He was holding her hand, and it was obvious they had just finished a lunch. A brown paper bag was neatly folded beside them on the bench (not scrunched up for the garbage can beside the bench, but to be taken home and put to good use again, I figured). They were both taking sips from the same small thermos.

After offering that it was sure a hot day, they moved over on the bench to make room for me.

The gentleman said this was a special day for them. It was their wedding anniversary. I have always thought when someone is obviously well beyond the three score years and ten, you can, in good taste, ask them such personal questions as "How old are you?" or "How long have you been married?"

To the first question, the gentleman said he had just celebrated his 89th birthday. Putting a dainty hand to his lips, his wife laughed and said, "Don't you dare tell her how old I am!"

They bantered back and forth a bit over their age, and then his wife told me she was a bit older than her husband, and that was why she didn't want to give her age. More chuckling.

I asked them what anniversary they were celebrating. "Our first," they said in unison.

After congratulating them, I asked them to tell me their story. I was itching to take out my tape recorder, ever at the ready in my parked car, but I felt I had to ease slowly into a possible taped interview.

We chatted effortlessly about everything. I introduced myself as a CBC broadcaster, and said I would be honoured if they would let me tell their story to my listening audience. At first, there was instant rejection. But when I told them their story might inspire other seniors to seek out companionship through marriage, they finally agreed.

Since this interview took place more than a decade ago, and they are no longer here to sanction my retelling of their story, they shall remain nameless.

They both grew up in a small community within a dozen miles of each other. They would meet often at Saturday night dances, so prevalent out in the country during the early twenties. But they "didn't have an eye for each other back then," the gentleman said. They both married other people, raised families and continued to live in the same area.

Occasionally their paths would cross. Although they both went to church, they belonged to different religions, and since social life revolved around their own churches, they didn't have much opportunity to meet socially.

"Tell her about the box lunch," the woman said.

The elderly man threw his head back and laughed. He told of a community affair, where money was to be raised for an outdoor rink, or something like that. He couldn't really remember what it was. But all the women were to bring a box lunch, which would be raffled off. The owner of the highest bid got the lunch and the privilege of eating it with the gal who brought it.

"Now, remember, we were both married with growing children," he said, his voice taking on a serious note. I was sure I was going to hear about a clandestine romance, or at the very least, a secret of a very personal nature.

"Well, the long and the short of it is, I bid on her lunch," he said, pointing a thumb in his wife's direction. "And I got it. Of course, you have no idea who brought the box lunch, so it was like buying a pig in a poke."

I watched his wife's face as he told this story, and I could see a twinkle in her eye, and a look of anticipation, as if she were hearing it for the first time.

"Well, let me tell you, it was the best fried chicken I ever tasted, and the chocolate cake and butter tart just melted in my mouth." Occasionally, the old gentleman would reach over and pat his wife's hand or her knee as he talked. "And that was that. I never thought any more about it. We both went our separate ways. My wife was the first to 'get away.' She died after a long and painful fight. But it was good marriage, and we had fine children, and I have grandchildren and great grandchildren.

"Then her husband died accidentally. It was tragic. I guess they died about three years apart, wouldn't you say?" His wife of a year agreed.

It was best to let them take their time in telling their story. So there were pauses, and I think now it wasn't that they couldn't remember the details, but that they wanted to get it right.

"A lot of time passed before we really got interested in each other," the wife said. "We were both up in years. We still lived in the same area, but we really didn't see much of each other for a long time." The husband threw his head back and laughed. So did his wife. I figured he had told this part of the story a few times before, because she seemed to know what was coming.

"I couldn't get that fried chicken, chocolate cake and butter tarts out of my mind. Even though it was a heck of a long time ago, my mouth would water every time I thought about that box lunch. I couldn't really remember what she looked like, but boy, could I remember that box lunch."

They both laughed and laughed, and so did I.

"So, you really married her for her cooking, did you?"

"Well, yes and no." They both became serious again. And took a long time to go on. They said there is nothing more lonely than living alone when you are up in years. They told of busy families, who had their own concerns with their own children, jobs and homes. They told of long evenings alone. But Sundays were the worst. They didn't get out to church as often as they would like, because of bad weather, sore knees, no transportation and, sometimes, because they just didn't have the heart to get dressed and get out. And that day of the week seemed endless.

Their children were supportive when they announced they were getting married. In fact, they had already talked to the minister.

Another chuckle. "There wasn't much they could do about it anyway." And so they got married. That was a year to the day when I met them on that bench.

We ran the story on "Radio Noon" and received tremendous listener response. It was decided that talking to people who were in their golden years, and who had warm, wonderful stories to tell, would become a regular feature on the show. Finding candidates could be a challenge, we feared, but as it turned out, once the feature became standard fare, letters poured in from children, relatives and neighbours leading us to special seniors they believed had stories to tell.

Kay Brookins

It was said that Kay Brookins heard only what she wanted to hear. Perhaps it was, in fact, her fading hearing, or maybe it was just because she was getting tired of talking about reaching the grand age of 99 and still in possession of all her facilities, that I was forced to go through a neighbour in order to reach her. It was common knowledge that Kay ran her own home, made her own decisions, and had little time for frivolous questions put to her by curious reporters trying to get her comments on the secret of a long and productive life. Whatever the case, it took me many phone calls before Kay got in touch with me.

Trying to set up a date for an interview was another challenge. Every day I suggested, Kay was busy. We finally settled on a date, but I was warned not to come in the morning, because she would be moving her irises that day! She would try to be finished by early afternoon, and I would have to be packed up and ready to leave by late day, because she didn't want to miss a ball game that was being televised.

Bearing all these conditions in mind, I set out for Pakenham, a quaint and historic little village in the Ottawa Valley, where Kay Brookins had spent most of her life. When I got to her lovely stone home on the Mississippi River, she was still in her "mucking about" clothes, as she called her dirt-covered slacks, straw hat and sneakers. And with one eye on the clock, and the other on this remarkable woman, I set about trying to find out what kept Kay Brookins so full of life when she was just about to reach the century mark.

Well, she kept busy. She was involved in her church, had lots of friends she saw regularly, and other "social commitments" that kept her running. Her beautifully appointed home was built by her father from reclaimed stones from the old Methodist church in Pakenham, she told me, and she pointed out the window to trees, shrubbery and the many irises that kept her busy when she wasn't running the roads.

Kay talked easily about what it was like living on a farm as a child. She went to school when she was five, admitting she was sent because her brother wouldn't go alone. "I sat on the teacher's knee for the entire first year," she said. She remembered how her father crafted toboggans, sleighs and wagons as playthings, and stopping at the sugar camp on the way home from school to get a bit of sugar taffy. "It was a good life," she said of those years almost a century ago.

She became a school teacher, and when she was 23 years of age, she met the man she would marry. For reasons she was unwilling to share, she didn't marry him until 50 years later when they were both "old enough to know better" were her words. But it was a happy union, and was to last many years.

When her 99th birthday was approaching, Kay decided she should do something special. She thought it might be nice to go on a walking tour of Wales. Without worrying about what people might think about such a daring venture for someone of her age, she booked passage on the *Q E II* for the trip over, and decided to fly home on the Concorde!

Kay took on a look of utter amazement when I asked her why she took the Concorde back. "Because I wanted to see what it was like. I must say, other than being in New York three hours after I left Britain, it wasn't that special. In fact, I would say it was grossly overrated, and as far as I was concerned, it was a washout." So much for that adventure.

Of course, I expected her to say her trip to Wales was one of the highlights of her life. But after telling me it was her fourth time there, I wondered what could top her latest trip on a luxury liner and the fastest passenger plane in the world. "That would be my trip to Switzerland when I was 97," she said, as if it was no big deal to go traipsing off to Europe three years short of your 100th birthday.

Kay loved all sports, but especially baseball. She had been disgusted at the teams during their recent strike. But not enough to stop watching the games on television. Her ambition was to get to the Sky Dome in Toronto, but she wasn't sure she could work it into her busy schedule.

Our interview ended when Kay Brookins politely told me I would have to excuse her as the afternoon was slipping away and she still had a few things to do before settling down to watch the ball game. I asked the standard question everyone asks someone who has survived close to 100 years. To what did she owe her longevity?

She said she owed everything to steaming bowls of homemade oatmeal porridge every morning for her breakfast. "And it must work," she said. Apart from a bit of arthritis, and admitting to fading hearing, she considered herself to be in excellent health.

When Kay's 100th birthday rolled around, the United Church in Pakenham hosted a tea for her. It certainly wasn't her idea, but she went and had a wonderful time. Hundreds showed up to offer their best wishes.

Kay Brookins lived another four years. At the very last, she was forced to move from the home she had loved and lived in for close to 80 years.

Arthur Ball's Love Story

Because much would be lost in my telling this story, it is going to be repeated here, exactly as it was told to me, taped for a Valentine's Day special. I had travelled to a small community southeast of Ottawa called Chesterville to talk to 91-year-old Arthur Ball about his love story. It was one of many in our series on older people who had warm and interesting stories to tell.

Arthur Ball's interview was typical of those in the series. With few exceptions, most were of ordinary people, but each one evoked tremendous response from listeners to "Radio Noon."

"I remember December the 13th, 1922, as if it was yesterday. You know, that was the day my life really began. I was only 21 years old, and on that day, I took Eurith as my bride in the Methodist manse at Elma. Today, any marriage that survives more than a decade is considered a long relationship. To be married more than 70 years seems almost beyond my comprehension.

"We are separated now, in a sense. But it's not our choice. It's because of Eurith's poor health. Even though she is in a long-term-care wing at the Winchester and District Hospital, it just means we don't see each other 24 hours a day anymore. That's what we were always used to, being together, doing everything together, and never being apart. But I go to see her every single day. I have never missed, unless the weather was so bad that I couldn't get out the lane, and even though I am past my 90th birthday by a few years, I still drive my car, so getting in to the hospital isn't a problem. And I would never miss those visits. She counts on me being there. That's the way it has always been...she counts on me.

"You know, it's hard to remember the first time I met Eurith, because I don't ever think there was a first time. It seems to me now we always knew each other. You could say she was the girl next door. We played together as children, we had the same friends, we have always known each other. We paired off as soon as we were old enough. It didn't take long for the people of Chesterville to know we were serious. Especially when I started taking her to the Saturday night dances, and driving her into town to sit on the main street in the car watching the farmers go in and out of the stores to buy their week's supplies. That was a big night. It was considered a date. Can you imagine anyone doing that today and getting a kick out of it? I guess not.

"We always did things together and we were best fiends. Even to this day, Eurith is my best friend. She doesn't recognize too many people, but she always knows me. The nurses tell me when I'm not around she often calls out my name. That saddens me, but the nurses know I will be there soon, and they try to calm her down and tell her, 'Arthur is on his way.' That makes her feel better. That's what comes from living under the same roof for more than 70 years, I guess.

"Now, let me tell you about that day in December 1922. It was a real blister of a cold day. There couldn't have been too much snow, because I remember driving to the manse in the buggy with the rubber tires. And after we got married, we took the buggy over to Brockville for our honeymoon. It was nothing fancy, mind you. Just a couple days away. There was no money then to waste on anything frivolous, and when those two or three days were over, it was right back to the farm south of Chesterville, and we got right into trying to make a go of it. And there were no words from the minister, either, on how to make a marriage work. No words of wisdom. No advice.

"But let me tell you, making a go of marriage was a lot easier than trying to make a go at farming. That meant that my new wife worked right alongside me. Back then there was no such thing as her work and my work. We worked together. I could never have survived the Depression without Eurith at my side. And that's for sure!

"We never had any children, and so our pleasure in life came from each other. I told you, she was my best friend. People often ask me what makes a marriage survive 70 years. I think a better question is what happens to a marriage if one of the pair has to move to a home to live out their life away from the mate they have known all their lives. Well, I'll tell you. You just go on like before. The only thing that has changed is that Eurith doesn't remember much of those 70 years anymore. But when I go in to see her, I talk just as if everything was the same, that nothing had changed. Sometimes it's hard. Because I remember every-thing as if it happened yesterday. Everything is as clear as a bell.

But I talk to her anyway, and I always tell her how much she has meant to me. How important she was and still is. I think she needs to hear that. You know, life would have no meaning without her.

"I know it's Valentine's Day, but we won't do much about it. I'll go and visit her just like always. We'll hold hands like we always do, and of course I'll talk about the past. Sometimes, if I'm lucky, that will cause her to remember something, too. I may bring her some chocolates. She loves chocolates. If she was like her old self, I would give her the whole box. But she can't have that many now. So I will just hand her a few, and we'll eat them together, and we'll talk about Valentine's Day maybe. And as I do every time I go in the hospital, I'll tell her again, that just because she is in one building and I am in another, it doesn't mean that we aren't together in our hearts. I'll tell her just like we have been for more than 70 years."

Wedded Bliss?

The directions came from a minister who, having heard our tales on "Radio Noon" of seniors in our listening area who had wonderful and warm stories to tell, suggested I talk to an elderly couple in the farthest reaches of the Upper Ottawa Valley.

She was just turning 100; he was 99. They were both hale and hearty and still lived and worked on their small farm, although I was soon to learn they didn't do much farming anymore.

I guess I picked a bad day to visit. They had just had a great and glorious fight. The husband welcomed me, but his wife of 80 years was less than cordial. She ignored me completely while her husband ushered me to the kitchen table and was more than willing to tell me how to survive 80 years of what appeared that day to be something unlike wedded bliss.

He started out by telling me his wife was a bit out of sorts that day. It had to do with the fact that he had just turned the farm over to his 75-year-old son, who his wife was sure would lose it because of her offspring's slovenly and wasteful ways. To show her disapproval, she continued to bang pots and pans around on the cookstove so that I could barely hear her husband speak. But he had agreed to an interview about his long-time marriage, and by golly, that's exactly what was going to happen if he had anything to say about it.

He was a big man, his wife the size of a minute. He and I sat beside each other at the kitchen table, and he never gave his wife as much as glance as he ordered me to "turn it on," jabbing his finger in the general direction of my tape recorder.

I was sure I wouldn't be able to air one word of the interview, because I could see it disintegrating before my very eyes. If he was going to bad-mouth his wife, I had no intention of letting the whole world know about it!

What he talked about couldn't have been further from the scene in that country kitchen! He talked in glowing terms of his marriage. How he and his wife worked together as a team and made all their decisions as a couple (I squelched the urge to ask him about turning the farm over to his son without his wife's permission), and how they were living in contentment now that they had reached their golden years after so many decades of marriage.

Occasionally, I would pick up a snort from his wife coming from the general direction of the stove. I knew without a doubt my microphone was recording every sound, and I tried not to think of the endless hours of editing that lay ahead of me trying to make the interview presentable.

My minister friend, in telling me about this couple, told me to be sure to ask him what he did every morning when he got out of bed. Because it was common knowledge that for 80 years, the husband had made his wife's breakfast and taken it up to her in bed. I thought it would be a wonderful closing—if, in fact, I was able to use any of the interview.

I said I heard he did something special every morning when he got out of bed. He threw back his head and gave me a toothless grin and a laugh that could be heard in the next county. "Yes, I do," he said. "I sit on the side of the bed, and I run my hands all the way up and down my body, starting at my head, to make sure I haven't broken anything through the night." It didn't matter what I could salvage of the interview, I was definitely going to air that statement!

When I was packing to leave, his wife was still banging around the kitchen. He walked with me to the door, and then he climbed onto an apparatus that looked very much like a lawn mower. However, this piece of equipment had an iron seat on it that looked as if it had once sat on a very old tractor. It had a motor which he turned on by pulling a cord, and the thing came alive with a puff of smoke and a thundering roar that shattered the pristine countryside. He climbed on, yelling to his wife, who by then had come to the door—and who had yet to say a word to me, that he was going into the village to get the mail.

Only when he started out the lane did I notice that the cart had four different sizes of wheels, which caused it to careen lopsidedly down the road, much like something you would see in a Walt Disney movie. Finally, his wife uttered a few words. Fortunately, my tape recorder was packed away. "Damn old fool," she said, before turning and heading back into the house.

The Right Place
at the Right Time

More Than Just a Coincidence

It would be impossible to number the times I just happened upon a good story. Unplanned stopovers, pauses in a routine, coincidental meetings, and any number of unexplained occurrences, opened up opportunities for some of the best programming I ever aired.

Just going around a corner in a road and spotting someone or something that I thought was unusual, tweaked my curiosity and gave me many fine interviews and stories for an eager audience always anxious to hear about interesting people and places within our large listening area. Spotting an odd-shaped silo sitting like a sentinel in a field, gave me the story of how the Scots came to that part of the Valley and brought their silo-building skills with them from the homeland. And again, seeing a couple of old silos being renovated, put me in touch with an enterprising young man who was turning his silos into luxury condominiums. Someone burning mile-high piles of cedar boughs far back from the main roads of the county, gave me the story of an off-beat industry that supplied one of the country's largest pharmaceutical companies with the ingredients for a well-known medicine...and the list goes on.

Every time I accidentally found a story, where at first none seemed to exist, I realized I was not in this job alone. I travelled with an angel on my shoulder. Time and again I was mysteriously led to the right person, the right spot in a road, the one house in the neighborhood that opened the door to yet another good interview. It happened too often to be chance.

The Vancamp Church

It was an oppressively hot day. I had met my morning appointments and was taking a pause before I was to meet my next interviewee. I was on a busy highway southeast of Ottawa, and had just finished talking with someone in the town of Winchester.

Pulling onto a side road, I looked for a spot to stop, tilt the seat back as far as it would go, and grab a few minutes to doze off. What seemed to be an old abandoned church, close to an intersection in the road, looked like a perfect spot to catnap. But I was surprised to see the front door of the old church open. Hidden around the corner was a car, and so I made the decision to stop on the dirt road, rather than boldly drive into the small churchyard and intrude on whoever was inside.

Tucking the car onto the shoulder and under a shade tree, I rolled the window down, tilted the seat back and was just to close my eyes when I heard the most beautiful music float out from that open door. It was someone singing. The song was "Amazing Grace," and an organ was playing in accompaniment. I had never heard such beautiful sounds before. They rolled out the door like the deep echoes from a cathedral. Staying in the car was no longer an option. I had to walk through that church door.

Inside, I came upon a scene that could have been from an old movie of the South. Standing in a long dress, shoeless, with her eyes closed and her head tilted to the ceiling, was a beautiful young black woman with her hands folded steeple-style in front of her. Another young girl was at the organ. They were in such perfect unison, it was obvious they had performed together many times before.

I stood at the back of the church, so moved that I found tears streaming down my face from the sheer enchantment of what was before me. Without any question, I had never heard music like it. I knew this would be an interview my listeners would love. Waiting until the hymn was over, I moved to the front of the church and introduced myself.

The black singer's name was Mureke Rwaramba; her accompanist was Sharon Adams. Only then did I look around that small church and realize that something was very strange about this building. It had been turned into a virtual musical cathedral! Pianos and organs filled the entire perimeter of the church. There were at least a dozen of every shape and size.

Who would fill an old church, out in the middle of nowhere, with musical instruments, and who were these two young women? As it turned out, there was not one story here, but three. I'll start with the church.

As luck would have it that day, the owner of that little church drove by to check on the building, and again by chance, I was able to talk to him about the building and how it had come to be filled with pianos and organs.

He said the Vancamp United Church had closed its door more 30 years before. The congregation had subsequently joined other larger churches in the area, and it was decided that Vancamp would have to be torn down so as to not fall into ruin. It was soon discovered that it would cost more to level the church than it was worth. When Roy Fawcett offered to take it off their hands for one dollar, they jumped at the proposal.

Roy was looking for a building to house his large collection of theatre and church organs and pianos of every description. He had a solid reputation all over the world as a superb organ restorer and builder, and his home was bursting at the seams with his stock of musical instruments. The church, he reasoned, would be an ideal place to serve as a showroom.

It would be many months later, and thousands and thousands of dollars in renovation costs, before Roy had the church fixed up to his liking. Today, it holds one grand piano, a large theatre organ, and 30 other organs of every description.

His expertise in organ repair has taken Roy to Holland, England, Jamaica and all over the United States and Canada. I found out much later that it is generally agreed that if Roy Fawcett can't fix an organ, it is probably beyond repair.

And so, there I found myself in this quaint little country church which had been saved from destruction. With my tape recorder rolling, I learned about the two young women who had so enthralled me with their performance.

The organist, Sharon Adams, lived in that part of Eastern Ontario, too. She had shown remarkable musical talent from a young age, and Roy Fawcett, quick to appreciate her ability, had hired her to accompany him on his trips for organ repair and installations. At the completion of his work, Sharon would give concerts, showing potential buyers and those whose pianos and organs were undergoing repair, exactly what the instrument could do.

Sharon Adams was considered one of the finest musicians in Canada, and her fame has seen her accompany that great gospel singer George Beverly Shea, who is a regular on the Billy Graham Crusades. And here she was, in a small church in rural Eastern Ontario!

But who was the young black woman who sang like an angel?

I discovered that Mureke Rwaramba came from Africa. She kept moving from one troubled area to another, finally emigrating from Uganda to Canada. She loved to sing. She had a rich, deep voice, so filled with emotion that one had to wonder how she ever escaped the New York concert halls!

Again, Roy Fawcett was quick to recognize her talent when he first heard her sing. She was soon doing concerts with Sharon Adams, and thrilling audiences all over Eastern Ontario.

When I stopped to realize the goldmine I had happened upon accidentally, I again was struck with the realization that I was not driving these roads alone. Someone or something was propelling me along, ever leading me in the right direction, telling me where to turn, where to stop, and pointing me in the direction of still another wonderful warm story to bring to my listeners.

The $10,000 Home

The interview took me to the farthest reaches of the Upper Ottawa Valley. This was unchartered waters for me. Oh, I knew the main roads like the back of my hand, but the directions led me through twists and turns and into an area surrounded by tall timbers, rail fences and bearing the trademarks of true pioneer country. I was there to talk about a set of maps and brochures a young man was publishing for the purpose of bringing some recognition to the area. He was sending these out across the country, and as well, he was putting out a magazine about the region which he hoped would attract tourists to that part of the Ottawa Valley.

While I was packing up to leave, we talked about his neighbours and the simple lives they lived far from the city, and how they relied on each other. And then he commented on how we all wasted money buying what we often didn't need. He remarked, "Take John Keith down the road. Now, there's a man who knows how to save a buck. You know, he built his entire house for under $10,000." I offered it must be pretty primitive and lacking in any of the modern-day amenities. "Not at all. He has everything anyone would need. But he sure knows how to make do with very little."

This sounded like my kind of story. It was the late 1980s, and everyone in the country was crying about the high cost of everything from rent to groceries to housing. One short phone call later and I was on my way to see what I expected to be nothing more than a shack, thrown together to keep on budget. I wondered about the wisdom of tracking down someone who possibly lived like a hermit, with nothing more than the bare essentials.

I was happy that the house was on a good road, at least. And then I silently gave myself a lecture about taking off on a tangent just because someone had mentioned in passing a neighbour who was clever enough to build a home for under $10,000. But I had phoned ahead (at least he wasn't so isolated that the phone lines didn't go to his house), and the appointment was set.

Told to look for a log house set in a cluster of trees, I scanned the lanes expecting to find something miles from the main highway. But there it was, sitting fairly close to the road. It certainly didn't look too primitive from the outside, but goodness knows what I was going to find behind closed doors!

John and Roxina Keith opened the door wide and greeted me warmly. One quick glance inside the spacious, open-concept home, and I thought I had been led down the primrose path. This certainly didn't look like a $10,000 home to me. It looked more like something you would see in a *Harrowsmith* magazine.

I wasn't about to waste my time if I had been misled, so I got right to the point. Did they really build their home for $10,000? "Well, not really," John said a bit sheepishly. Here it comes, I

thought. And me thirty miles out of my way! "The cost was really closer to five or six thousand dollars." I quickly set up my tape recorder; we settled into their warm and inviting living room and I listened to their story.

The house is made of felled logs, and every piece of furniture inside had its own story, as does every pane of glass. Furthermore, the house was finished and they were debt-free!

The Keiths started out with a fixed figure in mind that they were willing to spend on their home. Most builders have the same idea, but few reach that goal. For the Keiths, the absolute maximum was to be $10,000! Well, they met their goal, and with money to spare. Here's how they did it:

The Keiths started to build in the fall of 1990 on a 25-acre lot they already owned near the hamlet of Boulter, halfway between Bancroft and Barry's Bay. They cleared the portion of the lot closest to the dirt road, and the cedar trees they felled were cut into 20-inch lengths. Erecting the frame of the storey-and-a-half structure was their first challenge.

John joked that if he ever laid eyes on another pail of mortar as long as he lives, it would be too soon for him! It was hard labour, but they persevered. The logs were erected end to end in the stack-wall fashion, and from the road, the end result looks like uniformly sized stones. Between each log, of course, is that dreaded mortar, insulation and then more mortar.

Once the Keiths had the shell erected, the real challenge of trying to stay within their $10,000 budget began. Thus far, the only cash outlay had involved the mortar and the insulation. You see, the Keiths had no intention of buying anything they could get for nothing.

And this is where their story took on that wonderful human-interest element that every broadcaster is looking for. Their determination to keep within budget, saw them make countless trips to the local township dump. They crawled through neighbours' barns and back sheds, and kept a keen eye peeled at the heaps of garbage people threw out along the back roads or left at the end of their laneways for the local garbage truck.

John said the pickings were much slimmer in the country than they would be in the city. He said he was constantly amazed at what people threw out, as he pointed out the furnishings throughout the house that he had found in the local dump, along country roads, and hidden in barns and abandoned buildings. The kitchen sink came from the side of a road. All the doors and windows came from abandoned buildings and the township dump. Strangely enough, only a few were odd sizes.

The massive front door and antique panes of glass were once part of a one-room schoolhouse. A vivid turquoise 1950s-vintage refrigerator, now painted white to match the rest of the kitchen, came from a farmer's barn where John found it with its door to the wall. He said it ran like a charm and had never given them a minute's trouble.

As the inside of the house began to take shape with other people's castoffs, the Keiths were astonished at how items just kept coming their way. Discarded interior doors, old furniture, lamps people had considered beyond redemption…all found their way into the log house. Both John and Roxina put a lot of elbow grease into refinishing everything they picked up for free, so the furnishings looked as though they had all come from some exclusive antique shop.

They were particularly proud of one of their pieces of furniture. Salvaged from the local dump, their now beautifully refinished

Deacon's bench would have cost hundreds of dollars in a shop. It was all handmade, and looked just as it must have when one of the Valley's old pioneers had put it together some hundred years before. A rounded glass hutch was another find, but they admitted they had to fork out a bit of money for it. They both agreed they weren't above spending a few dollars, but very few, for something they found that had a decent price tag on it.

When it came time to finish the inside of the house, they did have to have the lumber refinished professionally, but they were able to cut a deal with the local Mennonite community for that. The same crew was also retained to do the basic plumbing and electrical work. The Keiths found their prices the best in the area, so naturally, they got the job.

They saved hundreds of dollars by keeping the interior of the house paint-free. Everything was left in its natural state. They considered paint an unnecessary expenditure, and as they said, it would throw their budget out of whack.

Roxina made or found quilts at yard sales which covered tables and beds, and she made all the window coverings, as well, from on-sale materials. She pointed to a brand new sewing machine. Considering it a necessary expense, she had no regrets about adding its cost to their total house expenses.

Another expense involved the purchase of tools and implements needed to put the house together. There were more than two thousand log pieces alone in the construction, all intricately fitted, and the Keiths considered they needed the best tools they could buy.

At the end of our interview, I asked John if he would ever again get into another venture like this one. He gave me the perfect close. "Only if there was some way to circumvent mixing all that cement for the mortar. The rest of the challenge of building a house and staying within that $10,000 was a breeze."

As I write this, I still marvel at how I just happened onto this interview. That piece was so well received that many listeners called for the Keiths' address. They wanted to see first-hand a $10,000 house, built by hand and furnished with treasures from the local dump.

The Inkerman Rockets

The interview was over, and I was heading further east in the St. Lawrence Seaway Valley. It was one of those crisp fall days, and I was taking my time driving through the little hamlet of Inkerman. I liked the name. Inkerman. It was solid.

I recalled hearing about this village many years before. The name rang a bell, but I just couldn't connect it with a person or an event. I pulled over to the side of the road, as I often did when I was deep in thought, or trying to come up with an answer to a perplexing question. Inkerman.

Of course! There used to be a famous hockey team here called the Inkerman Rockets! But that was 50 years ago, I figured. I remembered how everyone raved about this team, and how it had made a name for itself right across the country.

Was it possible there would be anyone in the village who just might have had a connection to the team, and be able to talk about it? I remember swinging the car around and heading toward the main street. Instead, for reasons unknown to me to this day, I turned down a short side street and looked at the houses. Which one would have someone inside who would be able to tell me the story? Heading back to the short business section, I retraced my steps. Again something propelled me to that short block of houses. I turned onto the side street, and feeling as though I had no control over the car, I swung into the driveway of a bungalow.

The man who came to the door was neatly dressed in a white shirt and tie. He had the morning newspaper tucked under his arm. I came right to the point.

"It's a long shot, but I wonder if you would happen to know anything about the famous Inkerman Rockets that used to play hockey about fifty years ago in this village?"

He smiled, I thought a bit wistfully. "I should. I started them."

What took me to the one house in the village of Inkerman, right to the door of the one person who knew everything there was to know about the Inkerman Rockets? Coincidence? Perhaps.

Lloyd Laporte was more than willing to tell me the story of that famous team and how he brought them from a bunch of rambunctious farm boys to a team to be reckoned with all over Eastern Ontario, Quebec and into the United States. His story was laced with humour. Sports certainly were not my strong suit, but the interview with Lloyd Laporte was full of the human-interest element I always looked for in an interview. Lloyd and I spent a couple of hours in his living room, and I came away with a story that is still one of my favourites. Here is what he told me:

Lloyd was a high school teacher in Inkerman, and he knew the kids well. The community was close-knit with a fierce pride and sense of loyalty, all of which would serve it well when the hockey team hit its stride.

Like all teenage boys, Lloyd's pupils were full of pent-up energy. In order to saddle that energy, he threw together a hockey team to play on the South Nation River. They had make-do skates, no one could afford anything else, and they played in overalls and plaid shirts with scant equipment. He coached them, but admitted to never getting on the ice with them. He did it all from the sidelines—the shore of the South Nation River.

Well, they got quite good. They took on teams from Winchester and other small communities in the area, and pretty well always came out victorious. They joined the league locally, and still without much in the way of proper hockey equipment, this bunch of high school village and farm boys began to be regarded as a team to be reckoned with.

Lloyd Laporte thought it was time they joined a bigger league. He knew they were ready. They began to have the support of people from all around Inkerman who would go out to every game and cheer them on. Further reinforced by the confidence Lloyd was able to instill in them, they joined the Central B League and beat just about every team hands-down!

Lloyd still never put a foot on the ice. "I'd put them out and they'd just take off. It was amazing the heart they had for the game. They were playing way beyond my expectations. And we never knew what a practice was. There was no such thing as getting together for on-ice strategy. Playing the games was the only practice they ever got."

In the year 1943, Lloyd thought it was time the team got a bit more organized. He called a town meeting, and chuckled when he said, "The whole 75 of them came out, and we still had absolutely no money. The village did say I could spruce up the team a bit, and they would keep a reserve for us if we went into debt. But we never needed to call on them for money."

It was generally thought that since the team was being asked to play farther afield, it might be a good idea if they had a name and proper sweaters. So far, there hadn't been a thin dime spent on any equipment, and the team didn't even have a name! Lloyd was able, through generous donations, to come up with $48 in cash to go into Ottawa to see what he could find in the way of sweaters so the team would at least all look alike when they got on the ice. Up to then, there weren't two dressed the same. "It just didn't look right for a team that was gaining in stature to look so rag-tag," he said, chuckling again at the memory.

With the $48 dollars in hand, he headed for the Byward Market area of Ottawa and found a sports store. He thought the name of the store was Rivers. He said he was looking for sweaters for a hockey team. Well, the only sweaters in the store that all matched were red and white with a large "R" blazing across the front. Lloyd looked at one for a long time, and then he said, "Fine, the boys have just become the Inkerman *Rockets*." The owner of the store gave him his entire stock for the $48, and Lloyd headed home with enough sweaters for his team.

The Inkerman Rockets began to travel miles around, and became so strong that they were fast gaining a reputation all across the province, into Quebec and as far away as Clinton and Utica, New York. In the year 1947, they played 35 games and won every one of them!

Lloyd began to get phone calls from all over...not only from other teams wanting a match, but from eager young boys wanting to join the Inkerman Rockets. Many of these new players ended up staying at the Laporte home, going to the local high school, and earning the grand total of five dollars a week.

Lloyd Laporte said of all the games, the one that gave him the most satisfaction was the one when they were teamed up against St. Pats in Ottawa. "Here was a top team. We were to play at the old Ottawa Auditorium, and St. Pats was so sure there wouldn't be a crowd to see this ragtag team from the country that they didn't even bring in ushers. Well, they hadn't figured on the loyalty of the Inkerman and district people. They came in every conceivable vehicle. It was soon obvious the place was going to be packed. Well, they had to hold up the game and bring in ushers to handle the crowd. And St. Pats was so sure they were going to win, that they had a bus waiting at the door to take their team to Montreal for a game the following day. Well, the Inkerman Rockets beat them soundly, and instead of *them* going off to Montreal, we went. It was a great moment.

"Then the team was scheduled to play a game with Big Jean Belliveau of the Quebec Citadels. Well, our boys played their hearts out, and did their best to keep Jean from scoring. But he was just too good for our young country boys, and he got the winning goal." Even though the Inkerman Rockets lost out, Lloyd considers that game on Montreal ice the highlight of the team's career.

People have lost track of those young players who made a name for themselves in the world of junior hockey, but the people of Inkerman will never forget the spirit of the community and the will to win that filled the hearts of those young rural boys of the 1940s. Ever since that interview, I have gone over in my mind many times the sheer coincidence of going to the one house in that entire community, where someone not only knew the story of the Inkerman Rockets, but had actually created it.

Velma

Opeongo High School was unique. In Renfrew County, situated somewhere between Cobden and Eganville, literally in a field, the school, under the principalship of Don Whillans, encouraged a unique approach to teaching. The school was going to have its senior pupils actually build a log barn as part of their curriculum. My producer was impressed. So impressed, in fact, that I was ordered out to Opeongo High School to interview the teacher in charge, the principal and a few of the kids, to see how they were getting on with what, we all agreed back in the studio, would be quite a challenge for teenagers, and a good story, to boot.

We couldn't have picked a worse day for me to head out. The rain was coming down in sheets, and at the last minute, it was decided I would not need a technician. Certainly Highway 60 was familiar to me. This was where our family farm was located when we knew it simply as the Northcote Side Road during the Depression. But I was most reluctant to go that day for some reason. I never liked to drive past my old farm. There were too many memories which I valued, and I suppose I subconsciously thought getting reacquainted with that area might change those memories and turn them into something I would no longer cherish. But I had little choice. My researcher had set up the appointment, and with the rain pelting down on my little Volkswagen Rabbit, I headed out for the two-hour drive, not entirely comfortable, but unable to put my finger on that elusive feeling.

The Northcote Side Road was exactly as I remembered decades before. There was Briscoe's General Store, and off in the distance I could see my old one-room school house, now turned into a community centre, so the sign said. These were the very roads I walked when I was a very little girl…three and a half miles of them, to be exact.

Just as I remembered, the ditches were full of water that time of year, both from the rain and from the early spring runoff. And as if I had turned the clock back 50 years, I remembered my little best friend Velma, and how we would tuck our skirts into our navy blue fleece-lined bloomers and walk in the ditches. Our mothers forbade us to ever submerge our feet into that icy water, but Velma and I did it anyway, carrying our shoes and stockings in our bookbags.

I wondered about Velma. Where would she be now? She would be my age, and certainly she would have married, probably a local boy, and had children. I drove on, looking for the road that would take me to Opeongo High School, not sure of where I was going, only knowing I was headed in the right direction.

I knew I should ask someone. Many farmhouses were close to the highway; I knew I could have driven into any one of their yards and asked for directions, but something propelled me on. Roadwork was underway along Highway 60, and in the pelting rain, the workers wore slick orange rain gear. Any one of them would have been able to give me directions. But I drove on. And then for some reason, which even to this day I cannot justify, I started to cry in the car as I headed west along the highway.

My thoughts were on my parents, both deceased now, and my little friend Velma and her wonderful warm family of German descent, who were our next-door neighbours as well as my parents' good friends. In my mind's eye, I pictured Velma's mother, whom we children called Aunt Bertha. I could vividly see her dark hair pulled into a soft bun at the back of her neck. I recalled her gentle voice and the German accent she put on her words. And still I drove on and cried, realizing I was hopelessly lost, and giving myself a severe lecture on silly sentimentality when there was a job to be done. I knew I had to stop and ask for directions. I had missed many opportunities to seek help, but at last I turned into a lane with a big brick house and a sweeping veranda. I pulled the Rabbit as close to the steps as I could get it.

Making a dash for the door, I saw someone looking out. She opened it before I could rap, and she said, "You look lost." I froze. She looked exactly as I remembered my little friend's mother, Aunt Bertha! She had the same soft speech and dark hair pulled back off her face. But surely Aunt Bertha would be dead. Or at least very much older than the woman who was standing in the doorway.

"You must excuse me," I said, feeling silly, "But you wouldn't be related to a woman I knew many years ago, would you? Her name was Bertha Thom."

"Yes" she said. "I'm her daughter Velma."

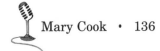

By this time, I had missed my appointment at Opeongo High School. When Velma found out who was standing on her veranda, we both cried and clung to each other. Velma and I spent the rest of the day sitting in her living room, reminiscing and looking at pictures in her album, some of which were of the two of us decades ago.

It was fate that took me down that lane from the highway, and fate that directed me to the one house inside of which lived my childhood friend. Because three years after we renewed our friendship, Velma Thom Stokes died, after a long battle with cancer.

A Funny Thing Happened...

Jim Turrell

Jim Turrell was one of the funniest men I ever worked with. He didn't mean to be funny. He just was. It wasn't so much what he said, it was how he said it, and the unusual things that happened to him caused much laughter around the studio on regular occasions.

Take the time I interviewed a farm friend about geese. Laurabell Henry lived out in the country, raised a big family of nine, often helped with the farm chores, worked in her church—and still found time to preserve, pickle and quilt. She was the kind of interview my urban listeners loved. She raised geese and chickens, and in our interview, which Jim Turrell had heard, we talked about the many uses of goose grease, and how it was considered a great household item back in the olden days on the farm.

One of Jim's distinguishing trademarks was the Wellington boots he wore to the studio, and he thought some of that goose grease we talked about would be wonderful to preserve and keep his boots supple. He begged me to see if my farm friend Laurabell could get him some.

In due course, Laurabell phoned me to say she was, in fact, able to render down a goose and she had a jar of goose grease ready for me to hand over to Jim. He was elated. Just what his boots needed, he said over and over again. And when he left the studio that day, it was to rub down those Wellingtons with the goose grease and give them new life.

When we arrived at the Château Laurier the next day and were getting ready for the show, Jim came down the hall on the seventh floor, and the first thing we noticed was that he wasn't wearing his Wellington boots. He had on a pair of ordinary shoes, and he looked far from happy. Of course, we all assumed he had treated his boots with the goose grease, and he had to leave them to "season" for a day or so.

"How did you like the goose grease?" we all asked. "Oh, I liked it fine," he said. "Unfortunately, my dog liked it, too. And after I treated the boots and went to bed, the dog ate my Wellingtons."

I would like to say we were all sympathetic, but we laughed so hard, we could hardly compose ourselves long enough to go on-air! Jim couldn't see a thing funny about the whole episode.

Jim and his wife Marilyn had a large family, and when he hosted the Saturday morning show, they were all young. Sometimes he joked that he would love to get away, just for overnight, to escape the confusion at home. Of course, he said, Marilyn would like the break, too. I suggested they go out for a night to my hometown of Carleton Place, book into the local motel, take their favourite books, have a good dinner and a good night's sleep, and hopefully, they would come back refreshed.

Jim thought that a splendid idea. And so he phoned and made reservations at The Twin Oaks.

Jim and Marilyn decided not to eat their dinner at an early hour, but rather they would read the papers in peace and watch television, and perhaps head out to a local restaurant around ten in the evening. They were looking forward to the quiet night and a nice meal to top it off.

Around 10:00 that night, Jim started looking through the telephone book, and found exactly what he was looking for: "Surf and Turf" on Industrial Avenue. Of course, he had no idea where Industrial Avenue was, so they headed to the main core of the town and got directions from a policeman. Their mouths watered just thinking of the lobster tails and the rare steak ahead of them.

They had no trouble finding Industrial Avenue. And in the distance they could see the sign "Surf and Turf." Within a minute they were at the place. And under the name, in smaller print, they read: "Repairs to motor boats and lawn mowers." There was their surf and turf dinner!

When Jim told us about it when he was next in the studio, he couldn't understand why we were absolutely hysterical. And to add insult to injury, there wasn't an eating place in town that was open past 10:00 on a weeknight. They had left the motel around 11:00 and driven back to Ottawa to their house full of children. As Jim said, "So much for our evening away." We all agreed, it could only happen to Jim Turrell.

Jim was just one of the many announcers who worked with me at CBO Radio in Ottawa. But he was one with whom I seemed to have perfect communion. We ad libbed our introductions to my pieces, and neither of us was ever at a loss for words. He was one of those announcers who always knew what to say to get us into the story I was about to tell. Jim Turrell gave me confidence when we closed the door to the studio, and I knew no matter what mishap might occur, he would get us out of it. He was that kind of a professional.

Embarrassing Moments

Mornings at our house were frantic, to say the least. With three school-aged children, Wally working 14-hour days at the store, and with me running the roads, it was a case of keeping to a tight schedule and rising at the crack of dawn.

Every minute was down to a routine. I would be the first out of bed, making breakfasts and lunches and thinking of the evening meal. Making sure everything I needed for the day was at the door and ready to grab on the way out, my day would begin.

This is how I made it work: I found that putting my undergarments on, and then only tossing on my outer garments as I headed out the door, was the best approach. By then, the kids would be away to school, Wally would have left for the store, and with one eye on the clock and another on the oven timer, I would head out the door.

One day that plan fell by the wayside.

Like all strategies, there is sometimes a glitch. The morning started out well enough, but if I remember correctly, I got bogged down with phone calls, a misplaced tape for the day's program, and a neighbour ringing the door bell to tell me my car lights had been on all night!

A quick phone call brought Wally running, and the car was soon humming in the driveway. I looked at the clock, and I had less than a half-hour to make the 40-minute trip into Ottawa. It was a chilly fall day. I grabbed my suede coat off the chair, donned it on the way out the door, and prayed I hadn't forgotten anything.

I admit it. I went way beyond the speed limit. And managed to slide into the studio just as a booked taping was about to take place. I opened my coat, which I hadn't bothered shedding outside the studio, and looked down at my body which was bereft of my outer clothes! Except for my underwear and stockings, I was buck naked!

It didn't take long for everyone in the studio and control room to know the dilemma I was in. Did anyone sympathize with me? Not on your life! I could hear the laughter coming from the other side of the closed door, and then my technician quietly came into the studio and turned the thermostat up as far as it would go! Within minutes, the perspiration was pouring down my face, and I was glaring into the face of my producer and technician who were enjoying every second of my misery. The suede coat weighed a ton, and I wondered how I was going to last for the duration of the morning. I sat for almost two hours in absolute agony, while everyone enjoyed my predicament.

And then, of course, I had the live show to face at the noon hour. Again I had to sit through the heat, as the tech controlled the thermostat to make sure I was "warm enough."

Mary Cook • 146

To this day, those who were on duty remember my embarrassment and the discomfiting few hours I spent in that studio. At the time, I wondered if perhaps I wouldn't be better off selling panty-hose in our own store!

In the end, the day passed without serious impairment to anything more than my dignity, and I went on to other calamities and mishaps. Only once did I really foul up with a program.

It was a huge special. It was all about a farm family from Western Quebec whose family had been on the same land for three generations. It was a story of perseverance, hard work—and what made the Ottawa Valley people special. We had given it lots of publicity long before the day it was to air, and I had spent hours at the editing machine in my home office to make sure I hit all the right highlights. Finally it was in the can, and I headed into the studio for what we were all sure was going to be one of those shows Alan Maitland had talked about: lots of human interest and listener appeal.

My technician put the reel on the machine to check the voice levels. He ran it for several seconds. Nothing. He rolled it back and started over again. The tape was blank! How could that be? It was there when I left my home office. I was stunned. My producer was frantic. Bill Kehoe was appraised of the situation, and in his usual quiet and in-control manner, simply announced that the program we had previously scheduled would not be available that day.

We always had a standby item, and it was inserted in the slot.

When I got home that evening, I rushed into the office, tossed a dozen tapes aside, and found the one that should have left with me that morning. There it was in all its glory. We ran it a few days later, and no one was the wiser as to why it didn't air on its announced day.

The last thing I always did when I put an edited tape into its box was write on the outside that it was ready to roll. For some reason I didn't do it that day. But I can assure you, from that day forward, I never missed checking the tape and the box it was in to make sure there was something inside for the listeners to hear.

Counting Frogs

It started out innocently enough. We were bringing in someone who was trying to build a Scottish community hall, and he was looking for some publicity to encourage city-wide assistance from the Scottish citizens who lived in the nation's capital. One of the kickoff events was an evening of music by the Alexander Brothers who were due to arrive directly from Scotland that evening for a live concert. We planned on taping an interview with them the next day to use at a later time.

The interview with the Ottawa Scot was about to start, and Bill Kehoe was already in front of the microphone in Studio H. I quickly scurried down to the records library to choose some Alexander Brothers music, which I thought would add an appropriate touch to the interview.

Just as I was about to pass through the control room, on the way into the studio, the Alexander Brothers stepped off the elevator. They had arrived on an earlier flight.

Quickly, my producer decided we would tack them onto the interview with the gentleman who was plugging the new community hall. Bill Kehoe was not aware of this last-minute decision, as he was already reading the news and getting us into the show. Ever the professional, he seemed not the least concerned when the Alexander Brothers entered with the Scotsman.

The show went downhill almost immediately. The first mistake came when Bill introduced the Alexander Brothers as the MacKenzie Brothers (from "Give me another beer, eh?" fame). He quickly recovered, and after acknowledging their proper name, he said he had heard them on some of their previous trips to Ottawa when they performed in the Red Feather Show. The Alexander Brothers had no idea what he was talking about. They had performed in the *White Heather* Show a few times, but they had never heard of the Red Feather Show.

I could see the show disintegrating right before my eyes. But the worst was yet to come. I jumped into the comedy of errors by saying I supposed they would be performing that night at one of the Sons of Scotland halls. Well, no. They were actually going to be singing at an Italian Restaurant in Vanier!

Bringing the Scot from Ottawa into this confusion, I asked him about the Scottish community hall plans which, of course, was the reason we were doing the interview in the first place. He mentioned the cost, which seemed like an awful lot of money to me. Foolishly, I voiced my opinion. He said he thought he would have no trouble raising the money and getting the entire Scottish population in Ottawa behind him.

I asked him how many Scots actually were in the Capital Region. Well, he didn't know exactly. They had never been counted. Actually,

he didn't think you could count them. "How could you count the Scots in a city the size of Ottawa?" he asked.

"Well," I offered, "if they can count frogs out in Lanark County, surely they can count the Scots in Ottawa."

My producer, I noticed out of the corner of my eye, was waving frantically in my direction. Bill Kehoe grew pale, and my technician was doubled over the panel board in the control room. Every button on my telephone lit up. I had no idea what I had said to cause all the commotion.

Well, apparently everyone thought when I said they had counted frogs out in Lanark County, that I was insinuating that the French population was being enumerated! I was, in fact, referring to the Ministry of Natural Resources who had recently hired a batch of university students whose purpose it was to actually count frogs wherever they could find them, because there was a real concern about their diminishing population.

Only when the studio calmed down, my producer gained her composure, and Bill Kehoe stopped laughing (and all the while our guests had no idea what the fuss was about), did I go on-air and say what I really meant.

By this time the damage was done, but everyone saw the humour in it. The story of my gaff hit the daily newspapers and it was still being referred to on-air a week later!

At the time, the majority of my technicians were French. We got along beautifully. They saw the funny side of the story, and the next day when I entered the studio, there on a wall upstairs was a floor-to-ceiling drawing of an enormous bullfrog, all dressed up in a red and green plaid kilt! Not one of those technicians would ever admit to the prank.

But it wasn't to end there. Listeners, who I am thankful also saw the humour in the program, began sending me frogs of every description. I got beanbags made in the shape of frogs, paperweights, framed pictures, and to this day I have a lovely stained-glass frog hanging in my kitchen window, a constant reminder of the day I unintentionally made "a racial slur."

Eating Crow

Harry Elton was the host of the morning show. He was an affable, articulate man who had made a name for himself in England as the very first executive producer of "Coronation Street." It is probably safe to say the show is the most popular ever broadcast in England.

Harry had also taught English in China. He was a popular host, and he and sports announcer Ron Wilson bounced quips off each other, much to the listeners' delight, who responded by boosting the ratings, making it the top listened-to morning radio show in the city.

One morning, Ron was predicting a sure loss for one of the football teams in the Canadian Football League. The game was between Ottawa and Toronto, and no one can remember which team was predicted to go down to great and glorious defeat. Harry asked him what he would do if the team won. Ron quickly said he guessed he'd have to eat crow.

Well, the team won, and Harry reminded Ron of his promise to eat crow. Of course, Ron assumed he meant him to apologize. Harry had another idea in mind.

"No, you will actually eat crow. We'll challenge someone to get a crow, and we'll have Mary Cook cook it." I happened to be listening to the news that morning from home and nearly fell off my chair. I had written a cookbook, but "edible crow" was not one of the recipes I had included!

A listener immediately phoned the station and said he would get the crow, and he would deliver it to Mary Cook. I got the call from Don Corbett, the listener, within minutes, telling me the crow would be arriving at my door in Carleton Place. I told him it better look like a chicken when he handed it to me! I knew crows were scavengers, and they ate everything from dead animals to cow dung in a field, and I certainly wasn't looking forward to having one's carcass presented to me, complete with black feathers.

The door bell rang within the day, and Mr. Corbett handed me what looked for all the world like an ordinary chicken breast, neatly encased in plastic wrap, and as clean as a whistle. I took one of my best pots from the cupboard, filled it with water, added the crow and turned on the stove. It was early evening, and I figured I would make a pie using my mother's recipe. Within minutes, the entire house reeked. The boiling pot produced the vilest of smells, and no one would go near the kitchen. But I was trapped. I had to have this "thing" down to the studio for the morning show in less than 12 hours. By the middle of the night, I still couldn't get a fork into the crow.

Digging out the recipe, I found that my mother added all sorts of things, including bouillon cubes, sage and bay leaves, to the chicken when she was simmering it. I tried that. Nothing sweetened the smell. Finally, I was able to pierce the meat. I cooled it, diced it, and began trying to disguise what it really was. Onion, a chicken broth made from honest-to-goodness chicken flavouring, carrots, potato and the diced crow were all put into a rich French pastry, and the thing was ready for the oven. The pot was beyond salvation. It went right into the garbage!

By the next morning, what seemed to be the entire city of Ottawa was accumulated on the seventh floor of the Château Laurier, including television cameras and the daily newspaper, all to see Ron Wilson consume this crow pie! The news even travelled on the wire to the West Coast. Knowing what had gone into the creation of the dish, I refused to touch it with a ten foot fork, but I heard Ron and Harry say it was just about the best crow pie they had ever eaten.

The whole exercise was just another example of the ends to which a broadcaster will go to bring some excitement to his show. In this business you are constantly aware of ratings and listener response. In those days (I think they have discontinued the practice), call-in sheets from listeners were circulated every morning, and they helped you keep a pulse on what the radio audience felt about what was coming over the airwaves. To have two or more callers phone to complain was a real downer. The day of the crow pie episode, almost the entire sheet was full of accolades. It confirmed once again that bringing spark into a program, and creating a bit of humour mixed in with the hard news items, was what the listening audience appreciated.

Sheilagh Rogers
and I ham it up

Alan Maitland and I
pose for a fan at the
Château Laurier

The Pebble Effect

In Print

One day the station receptionist called to say someone was there to see me when I was off-air. It turned out to be two young men who liked my Depression stories enough that they wanted to publish them in book form. At the time, I had given serious consideration to putting together a cookbook of favourite recipes from my mother's old cookbooks, along with those I had gathered from listeners throughout the Ottawa Valley. The idea of publishing my Depression stories didn't really hold much appeal for me.

The gentlemen weren't interested in a cookbook, and I wasn't interested in going beyond broadcasting my Depression stories, which I considered very personal, and which I couldn't envision in book form. I felt they would lose a lot of their appeal without the narration. We parted ways, but they returned and again pitched the idea to me. I still wanted a cookbook. They still wanted my Depression stories. Again, we parted.

And then they came back with an idea. They would consider doing a book of half recipes and half stories. I would have my cookbook and they would have their Depression Stories.

And so, in 1976, my first book was published by two young men in Ottawa, Paul Durber and Jim Irving, who owned the small publishing company of Opus Mundi. The hybrid book was an instant success, due in large part to the eagerness of Durber and Irving, and within weeks had to go into a second printing. The book also contained hints and economical tips, which probably played a large part in its being chosen in a *Globe and Mail* column that year as being one of the top three cookbooks in Canada!

The Depression stories being aired every week on In "Town and Out" were gaining in appeal every week. They were taken from my own life's experiences as a Depression child growing up on an Ottawa Valley farm, derived from 'mind the time' at family gatherings, and diaries. For the most part they were true stories; I used real people whom I had known as a child and added fictional characters if the stories needed them.

They were tales as told through the eyes of a seven-year-old girl, and their appeal seemed to be in their simplicity and honesty. Now in print, the stories took off. After that first book, seven others were to follow, all gaining in popularity.

• • •

Writing books was never part of my game plan. I would have been quite content to go on telling my stories over the radio, and having them published occasionally in local newspapers. However, as so often happens in life, you are sidetracked, or steered, in another direction, and you either go along for the ride or buck the flow.

For me, it was easier to go along for the ride. It has never been a simple thing for me to say "no" to anyone, or to any challenge. In fact, Wally has often said my tombstone will bear the inscription: "God called, and she couldn't say no."

A Toronto publisher, Deneau, approached me for my third book, *One for Sorrow, Two for Joy*. This book, again all stories which had previously been aired on CBC, caught the eye of a television producer, and it was made into a pilot for CTV. Although the pilot received rave reviews, I was never completely satisfied with either the portrayal of the characters or the storyline. However, it was all an experience, and I was not that disappointed it did not develop into what the producers had hoped would be a short series.

"Live and learn" could easily be the addendum to my fourth book. We decided to publish it ourselves. With no experience, a hefty bank loan, and more nerve than a canal horse, Wally and I published about 14,000 copies of *View from the West Hill*. Fortunately, pre-publication orders far exceeded our expectations, and the book became a great success. But the stress of promoting, selling, delivering, collecting the money, and the general labour associated with book publishing, was more than either Wally or I had bargained for. Wally still had a business to run, and I still had to produce my shows for CBC and manage a home.

And so I was more than ready to pass the workload off to Gail Baird of Creative Bound Inc. of Carp, Ontario, when I was ready for my fifth book. Since *Liar, Liar, Pants on Fire!* was first published in 1995, it has become a Canadian best-seller, and several of the stories have been printed in elementary school textbooks. Again, the stories are simple and seem to interest a wide and diversified readership. One would think because they take place in the Depression years, they would appeal only to those who are products of that era. Happily, that isn't the case.

My sixth book gave me particular satisfaction. Both my publisher and I were contacted at just about the same time by a man who had lost both his wife and his daughter to breast cancer over a very short span of time. He wanted to use a book as a vehicle for fundraising. Gail and I came up with the idea of pairing some of my Christmas stories with as many Christmas recipes as I could find in my collection, and put them together to form a book—*Christmas with Mary Cook*. A percentage of profits were turned over to a fund that promoted research, and it is satisfying to know that the project contributed even in a small way to the ongoing work of finding a cure for breast cancer.

For almost three decades, my narratives of the Depression centred in large part on the story of my mother. It was not my intention to delve deeply into her reasons for ending up on a backwoods Ottawa Valley farm in the 1930s, but only to superficially weave her story of survival, and the endurance of her children and husband, into the tales. The whys and wherefores were pretty much left to the imagination of the reader and listener. Why she came from New York City to such a remote and deprived lifestyle was never part of those popular stories.

It was inevitable that my publisher would want to take the stories one step further and tell my mother's story in book form. I was not enthused about writing my mother's history. I knew the interest was there, because I was constantly being asked, "What ever took her from the lights and bustle of New York City to the backwoods of Renfrew County?" But the thought of putting the story down on paper seemed to me a daunting task, and I felt I would run the risk of hurting some of the people around whom the story would revolve.

However, armed with a great deal of encouragement from my reading and listening audience, I set out on book number seven. It was the hardest thing I have ever done. I have said many times since its completion, that I wrote a chapter and cried a chapter until it was finished. It was my challenge to make sure that the man my mother married, virtually unseen, in order to make a home for two children, not appear to be a lesser person than my own father who died three months before I was born. My own father—educated, worldly and with an exciting career—and the man who became my stepfather—a backwoods farmer who had never been much further than the county he was born in—were as far apart as God could make them. And yet I felt I had a profound duty in telling the story to assure the reader that my stepfather was no lesser a man because of his lack of privilege. It *was* a daunting task. And I hope I was able to succeed. Certainly, the book has become a bestseller, and the rewards have come in countless letters from readers who have said the book answers many questions and fills the void left by superficially mentioning the circumstances which brought my mother and stepfather together.

Long before my first book was ever written, while the Depression stories were first being broadcast weekly by CBC, it was an editorial decision to refer to the man my mother married as my father, and the two children he took into the union as my brother and sister. I think it was a good decision, because surely, I never thought of them as anything other than my own kin.

Another Place at the Table: My Mother's Story took some liberties with dates, places and names, simply because so many of the people in the book were no longer alive. And there was scant detailed information available on my mother's childhood in Ottawa or her early days as a runaway in New York City.

However, the storyline is factual, and the book includes actual photos of the family and others. I think, had they been alive at the time of its publication, my mother and father would have approved of the book's content.

For reasons that often escape me, people want more and more of the Depression stories that have aired on CBC now for almost three decades. Perhaps it is because, in this age of upheaval, unrest and uncertainty, we are all looking for a more simple life. The stories allow one to laugh with, rather than at, the antics of countless people who have become familiar to my listeners and readers. They appear time and again, and many people say the characters have become like members of their own families. I could be paid no greater compliment. But I had reached the point where I didn't want to even consider another book. And yet, the book stores wanted more, because they said their customers wanted more. And so, I was coerced into another book. However, this one deviated slightly from the general theme. As well as Depression stories of the now all-familiar characters, I was asked to include introductions to each chapter which allowed me to express opinions and feelings, giving me yet another opportunity to reach my readership through a very personal channel.

These preludes to each section in the book moved me from being simply a storyteller, to another level. I was allowed to have an opinion on subjects about which I feel strongly, such as home and family. The book *In my Mind's Eye*, like the other books before it, has been well received, and when the final draft was sent to Creative Bound, I mentally dusted my hands together and said, "Well, that's that. I have just finished my last book. No more! Eight is enough!"

If nothing else, Gail Baird is a persistent publisher. She felt I

had one more book in me. She was keen that my long tenure with the CBC be recognized and a few of the stories told. And the way to do that was to write about those four plus decades, and how a very ordinary small town girl grabbed luck by the tail, and rose from broadcasting from a country fair to national radio.

This book has not been an easy one to put together. It was harder to decide what to leave out than it was to decide what to include. There are countless wonderful people stories that had to be sacrificed because of space. The decision of what to omit was painful, because in many cases, their stories will never be told. But it is hoped that the ones we did include will paint a picture of what some ordinary people have contributed to the fibre of our country, and how their narratives will live on in the hearts and minds of the reader.

Back to my roots

My one-room schoolhouse at Northcote

A busload of listeners are treated to a visit to my family farm

Signing books at Stanley Corners

Storytelling and reading at an Ottawa Valley museum

Okay, Mary, You're On!

n advantage, if you want to call it that, of being in the public eye in a relatively small community (as compared with Metropolitan Toronto or Montreal, for instance) is that you become very well known over a short period of time. By the time I had been doing regular programming on CBO in Ottawa for about two years, invitations to judge bake sales, participate in telethons and be an after-dinner speaker at countless events began to pour in. Although these commitments added greatly to my workload, I thoroughly enjoyed the contact they gave me with my listening audience, and the feeling that I was contributing even in a small way to many charities and worthy causes. In fact, I considered it an honour to be asked, and the advice from Alan Maitland years before still rang in my head: "Building a listening audience is like building a brick house. You do it one brick at a time."

My voice, which I consider strange, became a trademark. Even though, years before, the CBC had sent someone to rid me of my pronounced Ottawa Valley accent, it hadn't entirely worked. I never liked my voice, and disliked it more when listening to myself on playback. But the listeners liked it, and that was all that mattered. Soon, when I spoke in a store while making a purchase, someone would invariably say, "My goodness, you're Mary Cook. I'd recognize that voice anywhere!" And so, it is probably safe to say that my voice was as unique as the type of programming I was doing.

I don't think of myself as a public speaker. I think of myself as a storyteller who never writes a speech. It would be impossible for me to speak from a written script. I'm not sure it could be classified as a talent, but certainly I am much more comfortable 'winging' it, with perhaps a few notes to keep me on track. I have to admit that often I make up my mind what I am going to talk about on my way up to the podium. It must be working, because if you count the bazaars and county fairs I open, the charity appearances and after-dinner speeches, readings in classrooms, and visits to nursing homes, I give about 100 addresses in any given year. I often say, that number doesn't necessarily mean I am a great speaker. It more than likely means there is nobody doing what I am doing, and that is: storytelling based on actual people and fact. After 47 years of writing stories and meeting thousands of people who have led such interesting lives, my resources are unlimited.

These public appearances have opened up many doors for me, and brought me into personal contact with those who have been faithful listeners and readers for decades. There is nothing more gratifying than to have your work appreciated, and certainly it is that appreciation of what I do that keeps me going. These personal appearances, I know, are a direct result of my being a broadcaster. Had I not had the job I had, I doubt writing only would have opened up this door to yet another dimension in my work.

Speaking to countless charities and groups of people have given me many chuckles, and this book would not be complete if some of those stories were not included. My trips up to the podium have been varied and have covered a wide gamut of experiences.

Take the time I was invited to speak to a Women's Institute meeting one winter evening. The meeting was to be held at a small church in a remote part of the county. It was one of the worst nights of the winter with howling winds and freezing rain. Wally said I was a fool to start out. Being a product of the 1930s, of course, meant that a promise made was a promise kept, and I headed out over ice-covered back roads, barely creeping along. Eventually reaching the little church, I was surprised to find only one other car in the parking lot. The person who had invited me to speak said she expected about 30 people. I slipped and slid to the door, opened it, and found one lonely man sitting with his coat on, huddled around an oil stove that was dead cold! He seemed astounded that I came, and said he had received a call to come to the hall to turn out the lights and make sure the stove was off, because the president was positive no one in her right mind would venture out on a night like that! It took me almost two hours to get home, when under ordinary circumstances, I could have been back on my doorstep in about 30 minutes! No one bothered to let me know the meeting had been cancelled.

• • •

Remembering another speaking commitment always brings a chuckle from my husband and children. Once again, it was a

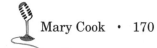

terrible night, only this time, it was in the middle of summer. With my dread of electric storms, I was very apprehensive driving off to a meeting 40 miles from my home with the lightning, pouring rain and thunder crashing around me.

As is often the case at a meeting such as this, awards are given out after the dinner, and then the speaker is introduced, which could mean a very late evening, depending on the number of people being recognized by the organization. I asked the chairman if he minded if I spoke before the awards, so that I could get on the road, since the storm was still raging outside, and I had no wish to be stranded on a back road many miles from home.

He agreed and left the table, I supposed to convey the slight change in plans to the person who was obviously given the job of thanking me. When that time came, the woman got up from her place and came to the head table, bearing a beautifully wrapped basket which I presumed was the usual basket of teas, cheeses and crackers, always much appreciated by my family and me.

I was surprised when she handed me the basket that it was as light as a feather. After a tortuous ride home through driving rain, I went into the house and found my family engrossed in a favourite television show. I passed the basket to my daughter and told her to open it, as I was heading for the shower and a nightgown. A few moments later, I heard uproarious laughter coming from the family room. I couldn't imagine what was so funny until I came downstairs and viewed what had been so beautifully wrapped in the gift basket. Inside were two Dairy Queen cups, two Dairy Queen spoons and a package of pudding mix!

My daughter, quite young at the time, repeated what I often said to her, "Mom, it's the thought that counts." Yes, indeed.

There can't be anything worse than being caught in a situation where you are ready to explode with laughter and unable to do so because of where you are.

An invitation had been accepted by my producer on my behalf to speak to a large gathering of seniors who were meeting in an enormous community centre. I arrived to find a long hall with the people assembled only at one end, and a single chair sitting right in the middle of the floor. I headed down towards the crowd to say my hellos, but was immediately cornered by one of the seniors and lead to the chair in the middle of the hall. It became obvious I was expected to sit there until told to do otherwise. At the other end of the hall was a shallow stage, and within minutes a kitchen band emerged from a side room and took to assigned chairs on this small elevation. The band included everything from washboards to brooms strung with wire, to pots being pounded with wood spoons. And right in the very front row was an elderly gentleman who was obviously going to play the bass drum. It was sitting on the floor beside him, but unfortunately, he had trouble staying on his chair, so when he started to teeter to one side, the person behind him would prop him back up. Likewise, when it came time for him to hit the drum peddle with his foot, the same man behind him gave him a hearty slap on a shoulder. He responded by raising his leg high in the air and pounding it down on the peddle, sending an earth-shattering din through the entire community!

It was all I could do to keep from falling off my own chair, but being in the very vulnerable position of sitting dead centre and alone in the middle of the floor, I had to retain some sort of decorum. I admit I could soon feel the tears welling up in my eyes and

I was sure that any second I was going to explode. Those who saw me trembling and teary, I hope, assumed I was overcome with emotion, because they gave several encores for my benefit, greatly adding to my discomfort. It was times like that when I thought I should have taken up accounting or basket weaving as a profession.

• • •

Meeting hundreds of people in a hall, some of whom I have met on other occasions, has always caused me great anguish, because I often have a lapse of memory, and sometimes can't even remember my own name, let alone someone I met five years ago in a lineup at a buffet luncheon.

However, I think now, honesty is the best policy, and that rule could have saved me from some embarrassment one night when I was guest speaker at a meeting close to my hometown. Knowing almost everyone's face but being often unable to put a name to the person, is a problem I am sure isn't unique to me alone.

While standing around talking to a group after the meeting, I was deep in conversation with a woman whom I had known all my life—by sight. I couldn't put a name to her face. Another woman came up to me and said, "Oh, you know Edith, do you?" Lying through my teeth, I said, "Oh, yes, we've known each other for years." The interloper continued. "You know Ralph got away, do you?" In all innocence, I answered, "Isn't that lovely, where did he go?"

"Ralph didn't go anywhere, he died," she said

Honesty. It always was, and always will be, the best policy.

• • •

Having to contend with a swooping bat while I was at a podium, enduring a session where the electricity went off and I was left standing in front of a huge audience with a dead microphone, and arriving at the wrong senior's residence for a speech, are all calamities which pale in comparison to the night I was asked by the chairman if I would mind if someone would say a few words on behalf of an Ottawa hospital before my address. I readily agreed.

Her few words went on for almost an hour, and then she introduced another spokesperson from the same hospital who also "had a few words to say." Her few words were another half-hour. By this time, the audience was dozing in their chairs, and I figured, rightly so I think, that no one wanted to listen to anyone else at that late hour. And so I simply rose, said a few words (*really*, just a few words) and sat down. Afterwards the chairman told me he expected me to be a little more "lengthy" as he called it. I assured him I thought the audience had been "speeched" enough for one night!

• • •

An introduction to a speaker, according to Dale Carnegie, shouldn't be more than a minute or two long. But I suspect I was given the shortest introduction in history one night when I was addressing a large audience of men and women, most of whom were strangers to me. The chairperson called on the individual who was to make the introduction. The gentleman simply stood up and said four words: "OK, Mary, you're on!"

And then there was the time the chairman forgot my name, and called me Betty *sans* last name.

Or the man who once called on me to speak by saying, "And

now here is someone who needs no introduction..." and that's exactly what I got!

Although I have done thousands of speeches in the last 47 years, I still am not totally comfortable in front of an audience. And I feel anyone who says he doesn't have butterflies in his stomach when he first stands up, is not being entirely truthful. John Fisher, Mr. Canada to those of us who can reach back in our memories of a few decades ago, was one of the best speakers I have ever heard. He gave me some sage advice when I first started out, and I have never forgotten his wisdom:

Always ask for a podium;

Always ask that the doors to the room be closed while you are speaking;

Ask to speak before the business on the agenda;

If possible, try not to have any close members of your family in the audience (they can unnerve you).

Public speaking has brought me in contact with thousands of people from every walk of life and from a host of international locations, including Singapore, Scotland, Ireland, Mexico, Germany and Greece. It is one of the rewards of being in this business. So many of the people I have met on this part of my journey have become lasting friends. I don't think of my speaking engagements as being apart from my job as a broadcaster and writer. I think they run in tandem with it.

...at the Glenngary Club, 1989

...with royalty, 1983

...the Chamber of Commerce in Athens, 1993

...celebrating fundraising efforts

...with the Wilno
Orchestra

...in costume

...in silly hats

...in tents

...and kitchens

...saying thanks

...and being thanked

 Mary Cook • 178

When One Door Closes...

Although there were many reasons why I left the CBC in Ottawa, none of them are of much importance to this book. What is important is that there was a life after that decision was made, and it came in the name of a phone call from "Fresh Air," a three-hour CBC show out of Toronto.

Going back to doing a weekly show was going to be too much of a challenge because of a heavy increase in my writing for various newspapers and magazines. And so it was decided that I would continue with my Depression stories on "Fresh Air," but only on the first Sunday of every month, a schedule that suited me, and that I could ease into my workload without too much pressure.

Leaving the show in Ottawa opened yet another door of opportunity for me. With "Fresh Air" being heard throughout the entire province of Ontario, rather than just within the Ottawa region, the listening audience for the Depression stories was vastly increased. The host of the show, Jeff Goodes, although young, has a sound appreciation of what his listening audience wants to hear on his program. The show is a relaxed mix of nostalgia and human interest and with an eclectic dose of music that appeals to a wide number of people.

The response from listeners who live in the farthest reaches of the province has been a joy to me, and brings the number of years for the Depression Stories to close to 30! Letters, calls and e-mails tell me listeners feel my family is their family. Along with me, they grieved for the passing of my beloved sister Audrey and my impish cousin Ronny, both of whom, for so many years, had been such a vital part of the stories.

With 47 years with the CBC under my belt—and 25 as an author—retiring should be on my agenda. Goodness knows, I have earned the right to do nothing more than sit in front of my fireplace and watch the ducks and loons on the Mississippi Lake that flows in front of my home. But when I give retirement any thought at all, I wonder what I would do to fill my days if I ceased writing and broadcasting. I have very few hobbies. I am completely devoid of artistic talent, and try as I might, I just can't visualize myself sitting at the kitchen table painting lilies on a tin can.

And so what I do is, in fact, my hobby. Seeing friends who have given up jobs they have loved, some of them trying and not quite succeeding in filling long days with meaningful diversions, confirms for me that as long as we enjoy our work, and are able to do it with some competence, retiring for the sake of retiring is not always a wise decision. But for those who can't wait to get out of the workforce, and who have interests to keep their minds and bodies active, I say, 'More power to them!'

Canada is indeed a land of opportunity. The brass ring is within reach of everyone who has the will and the desire to grab it. There is no doubt in my mind, accepting that all of us have certain limitations, you can do just about anything you want, as long as you want to do it badly enough. I had always wanted to be a writer. From the time I was given a cheap little red silk diary with a gold key when I was a very young girl growing up on a farm in the 1930s, writing was always a dream. Broadcasting was a bonus that came along quite by accident of my being in the right place at the right time. Both professions have brought me immeasurable joy, and I hope my readers and listeners pleasure, as well.

And so, as long as I can still put two coherent words one after the other, whether behind a microphone or in print, I'd like to continue doing what I have done for most of my life. And at the end of each day, I can say with sincerity and gratitude, "I travelled this way with an angel on my shoulder—and it's been a wonderful journey."

• • •

Also by Mary Cook

In My Mind's Eye
0-921165-75-7
$ 18.95 CAN

In My Mind's Eye connects past with present, as
Mary transports readers to a time when families and
communities were bound together by the need to survive. Mary's pres-
ent-day musings are interwoven with the remembrances of a seven-
year-old child, as she invites us back to the Haneman family farm in
Renfrew County during the Depression years.

Liar, Liar, Pants on Fire!
0-921165-40-4
$ 15.95 CAN
These were tough years for the Haneman family, but
Mary Cook's memories include even larger servings
of joy and laughter.

Christmas with Mary Cook:
Favourite Stories and Recipes
0-921165-51-X
$ 17.00 CAN
A collection of Mary's most requested yuletide
stories and recipes. This special edition is sure
to warm winter hearts everywhere.